Stop
Improving
Yourself
and
Start Living

Stop
Improving
Yourself
and
Start Living

ROBERTA JEAN BRYANT

New World Library
San Rafael, California

© 1991 Roberta Jean Bryant

Published by New World Library
58 Paul Drive
San Rafael, CA 94903

Cover design: Kathleen Vande Kieft
Text design: Abigail Johnston
Typography: G&S Typesetters, Inc.

Library of Congress Cataloging-in-Publication Data

Bryant, Roberta Jean, 1935–
    Stop improving yourself and start living.
        p.   cm.
    Includes bibliographical references.
    ISBN 0-931432-69-3 (alk. paper)
    1. Self-acceptance—Problems, exercises, etc.   I. Title
BF575.S37B79   1991
158'.1—dc20   90-22422
                                                                 CIP

ISBN 0-931432-69-3
First Printing, March 1991
Printed in the U.S.A. on acid-free paper

Dedicated to
Sally Hartley
Sponsor, Mentor, and Friend

Contents

A Word
From the Author

STOP IMPROVING yourself? What an un-American idea! Who is this Roberta Jean Bryant anyway? What kind of a person would suggest such a thing?

Well, I'm a person perhaps not too different from you—a veteran self-improvement junkie, a failed dieter, and recovering Twelve-Stepper. Since 1968 I've earned my living as an independent-learning and creativity consultant, lecturer, and writers workshop leader. Nowadays I prefer to describe myself as a freelance writer, freelance teacher, and freelance human being. My friends call me Jean. I'm both a rebel and a seeker who has tried repeatedly to alter myself to fit into our image-conscious materialistic society.

My frequent and futile struggles for self-improvement led to frustration and anger that exploded into fits of writing and creativity. I became weary of trying to please other people and never measuring up. I grew tired of seeing friends and students wasting their lives trying to live the way someone else thought they should live.

I finally figured that I'd paid my dues; I'd been involved with some form of ongoing self-improvement since childhood. I grew up in a repressive, one-parent family. Both my mother and the religion she chose assured me that if I could be good enough and improve myself enough, then everything would be okay. God would love me, people would like me, and I would be happy.

In my pursuit of perfection I bought and read every new pop psychology book on the market; I analyzed myself and my problems, and I struggled endlessly, but no improvement lasted very long. I felt terminally fat, ugly, and unhappy. By 1974 I'd been involved in a few encounter groups and a lot of diets, and I was beginning to emerge from depression and self-hate over what is now called an eating disorder. However, my preoccupation with compulsive eating or obsession with trying not to eat left little time or attention for my family.

My journey of futile self-improvement became one of active recovery when I accepted that I had a problem with food, and that I couldn't solve it by myself. Fortunately, I found Overeaters Anonymous. In that Twelve-Step program, based on the principles of Alcoholics Anonymous, I reclaimed some abandoned spiritual values, lost some weight, and became more fanatic about recovery than I had about self-improvement. I identified myself as an addictive personality who came from a dysfunctional family.

I compulsively joined every new program that came along and began teaching self-assessment workshops. I still neglected my husband and four children. Eventually my husband and I divorced; I experienced a brief physical and emotional breakdown, and gave up custody of my two teenage sons. During the following months of "shaky time" I began to learn to take care of myself, to rebuild my health, and to reevaluate my life. Much of what I'd thought of as recovery had turned out to be just temporary self-improvement in disguise.

Losing weight had obviously not been true recovery or authentic change, but merely the illusion of change, and that illusion had contributed both to my divorce and to my breakdown. Clearly it was dangerous to stop compulsive behavior without other changes in thinking, feeling, and relating to the world. Apparently, food was not the enemy, fat was not the enemy. Despite what society said, losing weight or being thin was not the solution. Attending Twelve-Step meetings was not enough; abstaining from overeating was intolerable without accompanying joy and well-being.

In the many years since then, my previously grim self-assessment workshops have evolved into joyful *Accept Yourself—Journal Magic* workshops. In those groups I've worked with substance abusers, compulsive gamblers, overspenders, workaholics, perfectionists, and codependents. I've worked with people recovering from life-threatening diseases and life-changing events.

Much of my other work has entailed guiding and advising individuals who were writing short stories, novels, articles, family histories, and poems. I began to see that any involvement with writing or creative expression resulted in self-disclosure, healing, and personal growth for those who struggled to tell their stories. One woman, grieving over the death of her beloved father, spent years working on his biography. Another woman, a cancer survivor, wrote an epic novel about a woman who triumphed over great odds. A diabetic crafted poems about "the black crows of fear." One short-story writer evoked the fear and uncertainty of growing up with an alcoholic mother. A paraplegic wrote about the rehabilitation unit of a veterans hospital.

These people actively expressed their recovery issues in their novels, stories, and poems. The impetus to write, to make sense of their lives, to share their experience, came from their unresolved problems. As people worked to create their stories, I watched as their resentments, their self-pity and revenge issues changed to a desire to reflect their truths and to help others.

Creative involvement had therapeutic value similar to that which happened for people in therapy groups or Twelve-Step programs. However, the emphasis on creating something, rather than trying to get rid of something, gave the endeavor a more positive focus. These aspiring poets, novelists, and storytellers taught me a lot about healthy recovery. I've since learned that any creative involvement facilitates healing, and that each of us in some way is recovering from something.

There is more to life than perpetual self-improvement, more to living than the frantic pursuit of recovery. Integration is the goal; the integration of one's fragmented self, bringing those selves together in harmony and cooperation; the integration of one's program into a life that is whole. Eventually you let go of identifying yourself only as an addict, or as a person with a problem, or even as a person in recovery.

In this book I will tell you my stories of self-improvement, of recovery, of relapse, and of true change. The other personal examples are composites—to protect the innocent, the guilty, and the merely human. This book reflects my concern for the individual, and challenges you to question the value of long-term involvement with negative-oriented programs or groups, and the frenetic striving toward superficial goals. Instead, I invite you to engage in the uncovering of your true character—that process of mental, emotional, and spiritual discovery that results in true change.

I trust these creative options for joyful living will empower you to challenge and to question as you learn more about yourself. Self-knowledge is often more difficult than self-improvement, but it's always more satisfying. What's most exciting to me is that the ideas in this book will lead you to the true change that comes through self-acceptance. I don't know whether you should integrate this material or just make it fit with everything else you understand. And that's not important. What is important is that you're able to use what you understand.

When you give up the illusory pursuit of happiness through self-improvement, you begin to experience the enjoyment of freedom. The concepts in this book also provide understanding for the friends and families of persons involved in recovery programs, as well as individuals who have identified areas of desired change, but who have been reluctant to join established groups.

It is important to know the difference between true recovery and temporary self-improvement. It's useful to understand the relationship between self-acceptance and true change, as well as how to stop giving away your personal power. It is possible to help yourself to creativity, joy, and well-being without compromising your true nature.

Read through the chapters to get a sense of what this book is about. Become familiar with the different ideas. Try out those that make sense to you—ignore the others. I encourage you to actively participate in doing the Creative Processes, using them for your purposes and adapting them to your needs over the next six months. Do only the ones that appeal to you or speak to your needs of the moment. Don't push, or shove, or coerce yourself in any way. Be gentle, compassionate, and accepting of whatever you find, of whatever happens.

After all, the whole point of this book is not to perpetuate the joyless quest for self-improvement, but to encourage you to upgrade the quality of your daily life as you help yourself to the freedom of creativity, joy, and well-being.

Foreword

I MET JEAN BRYANT, the author of this book, at a seminar in Seattle in 1976. I had just developed ARC (Awareness, Responsibility and Communication) Seminars, a personal growth series using Gestalt methods with large groups. She joined the core group of those who wanted to learn more, and we played together for a while, developing and presenting seminars in the Seattle area.

Those seminars helped people to improve the quality of their lives. Since then the market for self-improvement books has improved, and personal growth has become a growth industry. Recovery is booming. Of course it is still desirable to grow and improve yourself and your life. And for many, recovery from some illness or addiction is more than desirable—it is a necessity. We are fortunate to have more ways available than ever before that will allow us to recover, be better people, and lead better lives.

So, when we have recovered, have used those techniques, have done those practices, then we stop self-improving and return, all self-improved, to everyday life. Right?

In this book, Ms. Bryant suggests that, increasingly, we don't return, enriched, to living, but continue endlessly to self-improve and recover. Like a patient who becomes addicted to the drug that cured her, we don't, when cured, simply enjoy our recaptured health. We keep on taking the drug, keep on consuming—at increasing dosage levels—the substance that got us better!

We confuse means with ends. We set out on the road to self-improvement, and for many this is a valuable and necessary road to take. But instead of completing the journey, following the road to its end—living—we pitch our tents and start "camping out" on the road. We become committed to the process of getting better instead of achieving the state of being-in-good-shape.

I am a recovering psychologist who got caught in this process. Like many psychologists, I had to recover from the occupational risks of that profession—overemphasis on intellect and analysis-paralysis—and I do appreciate all the methods and help I received. I began to wake up because I stayed in friendship with many ex-patients and ex-students and began to notice that many of them were, after some time, significantly happier and more content than I! I knew more; they lived more fully.

An apparent paradox begins to emerge in this book. On the one hand, Ms. Bryant discusses very clearly the danger of getting caught up—even lost—in recovery or self-improvement. Then she proceeds to spend many pages presenting some methods of self-improvement—methods I know to be very effective, having had a hand in the creation of some of them. How can she justify this seeming contradiction?

But this is not a paradox. There is a distinction between self-improvement as technology and self-improvement as an attitude toward the self. The difference is not in what you do, but the attitude with which you do it. If you have the feeling, "I'm below par—not fully normal, not completely healthy in some way, and I am practicing these techniques in order to get to par" (or to normal or to health), you are in the recovery mode—the health re-gaining mode. For people in the early stages of recovery from an addiction or dysfunctional process, this is an accurate and appropriate mode to operate from. However, if all goes well and you work your program well, you do eventually recover. Does that mean you should drop everything that worked for you? Of course not; you may very well continue some (probably not all) techniques that worked for you.

However, now you can operate from a second, very different mode, the health-maintaining mode. In it, you operate from "I'm well and healthy—at par—and I notice there are some practices that work to keep me here. I will do these practices from the standpoint that I am fine the way I am and that I can increase the likelihood of staying fine (healthy) by doing these things."

Imagine two men playing tennis. One, because of some warning signs of potential heart trouble, has been urged to play by his physician; the other is there just for fun, out of his love for the game. So is tennis therapy or recovery for one and not the other? The answer depends on the states of mind of the two while they play. If the one playing on his doctor's recommendation is constantly thinking, "What a drag this is; how much longer do I have to play?" he'll be getting little fun and less value from the playing. Essentially, for him the tennis game is medicine, with all that that term implies. The other man, who is playing for the fun of it, is getting maximum therapeutic value from his game.

Ms. Bryant's advice would be, "Plunge in and play with these techniques, enjoy them—and probably you'll maintain your improvement and recovery without even thinking about it." For example, the Stream-of-Consciousness exercise in chapter five can have remarkable effect. I have used it probably a thousand times for myself, and it has been profoundly effective. But I used it essentially for fun. Forget the reason for doing these techniques and do them as an art form or as a hobby—for fun.

Watch the state you are in while you do a self-improvement procedure. If you notice that you are working at it, wondering when it will end, feel you "need" it, or think of it, however subtly, as medicine, you are in the recovery mode. If you hold it as play, enjoy the moment for its own sake, and think of it as a hobby, skill, or art form, you are in the maintaining mode.

Remember, a mind that is busy with self-improvement is just as busy as a mind full of worry—and a busy mind will keep you out of the moment, out of living in the present, no matter how virtuous the subject it is busy with. No doubt you know people who work at vacationing; technically they are doing what they are doing for fun, but their "let's be efficient" attitude is similar to the attitude of work.

I'm happy to see that Jean Bryant has continued on the path of growth, and that these methods have continued to evolve in her hands. Try them; they work, especially if done with a light touch, not with too serious an attitude.

After all, the key to successful self-improvement is essentially the same as learning how to spell "banana": It is knowing when to stop!

Larkspur, California

· I ·
Self-Improvement versus True Change

· 1 ·

Are You a
Self-Improvement
Junkie?

*No one else can give me the meaning of my life; it is
something I alone can make. The meaning is not something predetermined which simply unfolds; I help both
to create it and to discover it, and this is a continuing
process, not a once-and-for-all.* MILTON MAYEROFF

AMERICANS tend to be self-improvement junkies, obsessed with the quick fix, such as thin thighs in thirty
days and other fantasies. Only four percent of adults in
this country say that they would not change anything about
their appearance, even if they could. Out of that dissatisfaction
we allow others to dictate the meaning of our lives; we com-
plain about their interference, but react to the opinions of
every Mom, Dick, and Mary. "You'd be so pretty if only
you'd lose those extra pounds." "You'd be more successful if
only you were more assertive." "Everything would be great
if only you made more money."

Then we start trying to change. In the meantime we with-
hold acceptance or love from ourselves until the desired change
occurs. The silent bargain with ourselves goes something like
this: "If only I weren't so (fat/timid/poor) then everything

3

would be okay" or "When I become (thinner/bolder/more successful) then I can love and accept myself." This kind of conditional love is taught and reinforced by the educational and religious systems of our society, which promise us good grades and other rewards if only we perform well, behave according to a certain standard, or look a certain way.

The proliferation of programs, workshops, and trainings compounded by the glut of self-improvement books, tapes, and videos is proof of this national obsession with self-improvement. The addiction to improving oneself, the search for perfection, has become a joyless merry-go-round powered by perpetual dissatisfaction.

These societal demands and expectations were fueled primarily by the tenets of church and family. But increasingly, the natural human desire to be the best we can be is exploited by Madison Avenue and Hollywood. There's nothing wrong with wanting to do well and to look good. However, when the advertising profession and the entertainment industry dictate standards and we succumb to those influences, we often violate our true nature. Christie Brinkley, Jane Fonda, and Tom Cruise provide superficial and unrealistic goals for our aspirations. When we choose movie stars, best-selling authors, and sports celebrities as models for how and what and who we should be, true satisfaction disappears.

The Resentment Factor

Healthy self-betterment, on the other hand, always results in increased satisfaction and increased quality of life. Self-improvement that ignores the individual's true nature gives rise to resentment. For instance, many expensive treatment programs for serious problems such as alcoholism, smoking, or drug abuse specialize in aversion therapy; mild electrical shocks or induced nausea are coupled with brainwashing techniques. Often the participants are there due to pressure from employers or family members, and their medical insurance picks up the bill. Resentment often follows when people are made to feel like naughty children receiving punishment.

Many other programs, such as those for the overweight, seek to modify the perceived problem in less drastic ways. The problem is usually defined as being too fat or too heavy. Programs and diets that celebrate weight loss imply that being thinner is *true change*. True change, however, results in a healthy relationship with food; dieting only perpetuates an obsessive-compulsive relationship with food.

Many people involved in therapy groups or support programs are motivated in part by guilt or duty or the desire to avoid further pain and problems, not by a real desire to change. Therefore, what they seek and temporarily find is self-improvement coupled with resentment, not recovery or true change. Self-improvement is based on the illusion, or theory, of improvability or possible change.

Judith's Story

Judith, a graphic artist, came from a strict religious home. High standards were set for performance and behavior. She became a self-improvement junkie as a teenager, and obsessively kept long lists of things about herself to improve. By the time she reached her early thirties, she had used her personal journal as a form of self-abuse, always finding herself falling short of her stringent goals. Her quality of life declined as she berated herself daily for not improving more or faster.

Every year after Christmas she did an exhaustive self-analysis, evaluating her performance in all the areas of her life: mother, wife, homemaker, freelance artist, citizen in the community. She graded herself as if she were still in parochial school—never did she merit an A. To compound this negative focus, every January she made a long list of strict New Year's resolutions. By February she usually had broken every resolution in some respect, and March overflowed with remorse and self-recrimination.

Judith, who was a fat teenager, became thin through bulimic bingeing-and-purging. When this sick involvement with food threatened her health and her marriage, she became involved with a therapy group. However, she used group pressure to continue punishing herself. Her failure to do things perfectly created feelings of guilt.

As long as Judith thought her problem was overeating or bulimia, she kept herself from identifying and dealing with her real problems. Her unacknowledged issues were perfectionism, low self-esteem, and self-rejection.

These issues underlie many problems and are part of what is now referred to as codependency. Codependency is the newest kid on the addictions block. It has been defined by the Conference on Codependency as "a pattern of painful dependence on compulsive behaviors and on approval from others in an attempt to find safety, self-worth and identity." Judith's codependency issues were masked by the focus on her eating behavior.

Eating disorders like Judith's are increasingly difficult to treat effectively because the societal emphasis on thinness assumes that fat is the problem. Fear of fatness has produced a national epidemic of bulimic behavior; bulimics become fixated on unrealistic standards of thinness and reject not only themselves, but the food they eat. Overweight is seen as such a terrible affliction that losing weight by any means possible is preferable to being fat. Even some of the other members of Judith's therapy group thought it was better to be thin and bulimic than fat.

Dieting Is Image Management

The number-one form of self-improvement in America today is dieting. When the primary aim of dieting is just to lose pounds or to look thinner, the goal remains superficial. On the other hand, if the goal is to achieve better health or to feel better, then changing one's eating habits can be a realistic and positive action.

Unfortunately, many programs not only promote superficial goals for unhappy fat people, but also reinforce underlying problems such as people-pleasing or "stuffing" angry feelings. The unspoken message is that you can best please the instructor and the other people in the program by following the plan and losing weight. This kind of weight loss turns unhappy fat people into unhappy thin people.

Dieting can also sabotage relationships with family members and well-meaning friends. Sometimes friends and family collaborate to keep the compulsive person from eating between meals or from eating potato chips or ice cream. That uneasy bargain relies on the concerned person's ability to play watchdog, which not only encourages irresponsibility by the person on the diet but produces feelings of resentment, deprivation, and loss. Deprivation, in turn, creates a powerful need that often compels the dieter back to the former source of solace and compounds the problem. What's really lost is self-respect, trust, and friendship.

Despite its history of failure to produce lasting results, dieting retains its power as a panacea because it produces a visible change that masquerades as real change. Dieters receive an unusual amount of attention until they begin looking normal. When the praise from others wanes, dieters don't know what to do for an encore. Dieting also maintains a preoccupation with food and eating behavior. In terms of time and attention, there is little difference between the obsession with food and eating that results in overweight and obesity, and the obsessive focus on calories and not-eating that results in weight loss.

Losing Weight Is the Illusion of Change

Losing weight is a false goal, a goal that masks real problems, but it's a goal that does create the illusion of change. Weight loss, however, is only movement, not real change, unless there has been a fundamental change in the physical or mental involvement with food, eating, and weight. If no change in the dynamics or relationship between the person and the real problem happens, then relapse is inevitable. When food is seen as a friend, an enemy, or a comforter, when fear of certain foods dominates, or fear of being fat is obsessive, then no real change occurs.

Real change for a person with an eating disorder reflects a healthy attitude toward food—enjoying moderate eating, seeing food primarily as a source of energy and secondarily as a source of pleasure. The struggle would be over and the conflict would disappear. No willpower would be needed to control eating behavior and the preoccupation with the numbers on the scale would fade.

The illusion of change coupled with the lack of true change explains why the relapse rate is so high for the overweight. It has been said that more than eighty percent of those who lose weight are doomed to regain it. Self-improvement of this kind is usually superficial and often temporary. Relapse is always the default position: when willpower or the vigilance of others fails, as it is bound to do, the old habits and patterns of coping by overeating reassert themselves.

Sometimes relapse is postponed by focusing the obsessive thinking or compulsive behavior elsewhere. For example, self-improvement itself can become a kind of addiction. (Some people carry this lust for attention into expensive rounds of cosmetic surgery.) Other addictions for the person who dieted successfully can include compulsive spending, shopping, or exercising. Addictive behavior regarding sex or relationships can also follow binges of dieting.

True change, unlike self-improvement, is a process of education—finding out about yourself, discovering your true character, and uncovering your true personality. Throughout the true-change process you examine what you think, feel, and believe. You challenge and sometimes discard some things you assumed to be true taught by your parents, friends, teachers, and other educational or religious influences. You examine things you read in magazines and books and saw on television and videos. Sometimes even the useful things you learned in therapy programs or support groups must be challenged; if they survive the challenge, then they are yours and worth keeping.

> *Self-improvement which ignores the individual's true nature gives rise to resentment.*

Getting Hooked on Support Groups

People with self-improvement or recovery issues tend to go from the extreme of denial ("I do not have an eating disorder. Everything is just fine.") to the opposite extreme of not only identifying with the problem ("I am a compulsive overeater") but overidentifying: they view themselves and their world through addiction-colored glasses. All they see are compulsive people, systems, behavior, and new areas for self-improvement.

My secretary, Katy, an est graduate who was involved with one self-improvement program after another, always remained cheerful. Although her perpetual cheerfulness bothered me at first, after several years I looked forward to her unfailingly sunny attitude. One day she showed up for work in a vile mood. "What's wrong?" I asked.

"I finally gave up chocolate," she said, explaining that she had maintained her happy disposition even while quitting smoking through the use of chocolate as a mood-elevator. She was experiencing withdrawal from the sugar- and caffeine-high induced by chocolate. Katy, now identifying herself as a chocoholic, had found a dramatic new focus for self-improvement.

Judith, on the other hand, after many years in therapy during which she avoided bulimic behavior, still identified herself as a compulsive overeater and bulimic. When new friends remarked on how attractive she was, Judith quickly whipped out her "fat" pictures to show how heavy she used to be. Her whole orientation still revolved around having been fat, and she remained obsessed by her eating behavior, past and present. It was as if she had no other identity. "My name is Judith and I'm a compulsive overeater and bulimic" had evolved into an unconscious "I am an obsessive-compulsive person. I am this disease."

Twelve-Step programs such as AA and OA, which perpetuate the disease-model of addiction, have recently proliferated; there's a Twelve-Step group for just about every kind of human behavior. Many people start out in one program and, when their primary addiction is under control, immediately begin identifying other areas for improvement. Cross-addictions begin when the underlying issues of the primary addiction are ignored. Many who chase from one program to another would be well-advised to spend their time and energy in one program, seeking to uncover the thoughts and feelings that lie behind the problem, rather than seeking more group support and a different focus for self-improvement.

In addition, some people may benefit if they stop compulsively running around to quite so many groups and meetings and become comfortable with their loneliness—that existential loneliness that comes from being human. However, one of the attractions of recovery groups is the notion that "you are not alone." And that is true; it is good to know that our problems are common ones—that others have gone through similar ordeals and have not only survived but have thrived and prospered.

Nevertheless, it's equally important both to understand and to accept that no other person can ever really know what it's like to be you. Even if you have experienced the same kinds of problems as someone else, your thoughts and feelings and the way you have integrated the experiences are individual. The paradox is that as human beings we *are* alone, but that we do not have to fear that aloneness if we have others with whom to share our stories.

We do need to stop and tune into ourselves more often, even though this idea seems alien to our gregarious culture.

The ability and willingness to be alone, to be lonely, even, gives us the strength to endure the difficult times that happen in any human life, to face the fact that no one else can ever really know or fully understand the reality of another person.

Fred, a thirty-two-year-old carpenter and recovering alcoholic, found that when loneliness overwhelmed him, no amount of human contact or distraction could really make it better. Fred learned to surrender to the loneliness and immersed himself in the feelings. Often he would turn out all the lights, crawl into bed, and concentrate on feeling lonely. Seldom did the feelings last after he began to pay total attention to them; after a while his feelings would change to ones of sadness, or anger, or boredom. As he started identifying what he was feeling, or as he began feeling better, he'd get out of bed, get dressed, and start doing something different.

Sometimes, however, it can be useful to know that meetings and other resources are available when you need to be with people. I think of it as needing a babysitter. When I need to be babysat, I call one of my friends or even one of my children, and say, "Can I come over and watch television? I don't want to talk; I just need to be with someone."

In the beginning stages of recovery from loss, trauma, injury, alcoholism, or a destructive behavior pattern, the focus is on how to recover day by day. Twelve-Step groups can be important during this time. After the initial period of recovery, however, it becomes imperative to shift the focus from needing to recover from this terrible thing to attaining that better state you seek.

It's important to move beyond false goals such as being thin or not drinking to positive goals such as a healthy relationship with food or enthusiastic sobriety. Then the next step is to focus on increasing positive involvement with life not recovery *from* depression, for instance (although depression can have a physical component), but recovery *of* self-esteem, joy, creativity, and well-being. Recovery *of* health, not recovery *from* illness, needs to be the goal.

Occasionally a product I use and enjoy comes out in a "New

and Improved" version; usually I don't like it as well. The older I get the less I want to be new and improved. More and more I seek simply to risk being fully who I am.

The following process can help you determine some of your true values and figure out what you are really seeking.

Creative Process #1
What Are You Seeking?

As you begin this process, avoid thinking too much about what you think the answers should be. Jot down the first things that pop into your head. Remember that there are no right or wrong answers here.

1. Make a list of six to twelve things you've tried to improve about yourself in the last few years. Include the areas that you feel in conflict with yourself. Perhaps Judith's list might mention all the things she tried to do to improve her appearance. Fred might list his conflict about how to socialize without drinking.

2. Pick one or two things on the list and ask yourself what you are really seeking, what lies beneath your goals. Judith, for instance, sought love and approval through being attractive; Fred's list reflected his desire for better health and good relationships.

3. Without thinking about it too much, make another list of a few things that fascinate, console, and preoccupy you—the things that keep you from relating to yourself at a deeper level. Judith listed shopping the mall and reading paperback romances; Fred's were watching television and driving around by himself in his truck.

Consider your lists as information only. They will come in handy for other Creative Processes in this book.

I don't know when you'll decide to use this material or how you'll make it work for you. What's most important is that you find value in your individual application and don't use it to make yourself feel bad or guilty, or to create new perfectionistic standards for self-improvement.

Perfection Is Not Attainable

Perfectionistic standards, like Judith's, and engaging in self-improvement to please others are among the factors that create escalating demands to do more and to be more. But there's never a point at which anyone can improve sufficiently to feel perfect; if perfection is the goal, no amount of improvement is ever enough. Changing to please someone else functions like emotional blackmail. As Fred learned, after he completed one desired change, more was demanded: after he stopped drinking, his family pressured him to stop smoking. The ante always goes up when self-improvement disguised as recovery becomes the issue in a power struggle.

The loser in these struggles is the person who can't stop improving, when the desire to be better and better feeds compulsive or obsessive tendencies. One form of compulsion manifests when coping mechanisms that make people feel better temporarily, such as buying a new dress or eating chocolate, become unthinking habits and individuals lose the ability to control their actions. An old Czech proverb states, "A habit is a shirt made of iron." That which you worship with your time, money, energy, and attention becomes your god.

Compulsion means experiencing no choice or control over repetitive physical behavior. For instance, physical exercise produces endorphins, a natural morphinelike substance. Compulsive exercisers can become addicted to these endorphins and can manifest physical withdrawal symptoms if they stop exercising.

Even after physical withdrawal is over, many people in recovery remain addicted to crisis and high drama; they are hooked on their own adrenaline—to intensity. This physical

and emotional component of the recovery process is often ignored when the focus remains on change of behavior or self-
improvement. Even support groups can feed that preoccupation, as participants get hooked on other people's stories and
crises week after week.

Obsession means experiencing no control over repetitive
patterns of thinking. Many compulsive overeaters, for example, can't stop thinking about food and eating. People who
spend many of their waking hours fantasizing, worrying, or
thinking about a particular event, person, or situation are said
to be obsessed if they can't stop themselves.

The unfortunate downside of an addictive, compulsive, or
obsessive preoccupation with self-improvement is not only the
financial drain but also the strengthening of self-rejection or
even self-hate. To engage in self-improvement requires judging yourself as not okay. The individual who truly feels okay
has no need to constantly improve.

In addition, this self-improvement mania results in giving
one's power away to authors, teachers, therapists, celebrities,
and other promise-them-anything gurus. When we allow
someone else to define how we should look or behave, the
resulting focus on self-improvement to please others obscures
and perpetuates what may be the real problem—often a lack
of self-esteem.

Aaron's Story

My good friend Aaron, for example, grew up in a family that
failed to nurture him properly; the kind of family that is
now called dysfunctional. Dysfunctional is an imprecise term,
because every person, family, and relationship has its dysfunctional aspects. Children in dysfunctional families learn to
cope; they study the adults and the adult systems in their lives
and adjust to those circumstances. Being dysfunctional is like
driving a car that has no operable reverse gear; instead of get-

ting the car fixed, the driver learns to find parking places where backing out is not necessary.

Although Aaron's mother and older sister were not alcoholic, Aaron had many of the symptoms of Adult Children of Alcoholics. He became convinced that he was a terrible person. Because he didn't know what normal behavior was and couldn't trust anyone in his family, he became a perfectionist who needed to be right and always in control. He spent much of his adult life adjusting to unreasonable circumstances; he chronically worried about getting into trouble and was over-concerned about what other people thought.

He prided himself on being alert and self-reliant—his body was tense, ready for trouble. Rather than awareness and responsibility, Aaron had wariness, anxiety, and rigidity. He thought responsibility meant doing everything himself; he never asked for help and was suspicious of any that was offered. He didn't realize that responsibility means "ability to respond," which includes being able to ask for and receive help.

People like Aaron find it difficult to fully participate in therapy or recovery programs, not only because of fierce independence but also because of distrust of anything they can't control. Aaron decided to diagnose and treat his own recovery issues by reading all the available literature on the subject; each book gave him a new focus for self-improvement. But his perfectionism and perceived failures at self-improvement interfered with true recovery and true change.

Another barrier was Aaron's constant deferral to other people out of a need for approval. He prided himself on being a good listener, but also frequently complained, "I can't get a word in edgewise." That complaint presumed that it was the other person's responsibility to take care of Aaron by making sure he got equal time to contribute to the conversation.

Aaron's focus for recovery, his self-diagnosed problems, were his need for pleasing people and his self-pity. But his silent demands that others be as polite and considerate as he was and his passivity about speaking up when he did have something to say created stress and resentment in his relation-ships. When he did make a request, it carried the intensity of a demand, the silent message being, "I ask so little; I'll be hurt or angry if you don't cooperate."

Silent messages and demands reflect the tyranny of needing understanding from significant others. An invitation or re-quest becomes a demand when there's a substantial penalty for noncompliance. When sulking, silent martyrdom, or sarcasm follows the other's polite refusal, it signals the need for ap-proval through manipulation. The tragedy here is that the need for everyone's approval means sacrificing one's self. After a while it's impossible to tell the difference between the ma-nipulator and the manipulatee; both are controlled by the is-sue of who will please whom.

Trying to please everybody guarantees personal unhappi-ness. Trying to please someone who needs to be in control often creates an escalation of demands. And conversely, depen-dency on pleasing others—the need to be loved and approved of by everyone—always results in more problems.

Food for Thought

The following end-of-chapter questions to consider as you travel the path of self-discovery are not intended to be an-swered formally or taken too seriously. Perhaps there are no real answers to questions like these. Approach them casually. Be playful, flippant, or even cynical. Allow a smile or shiver of recognition to furnish food for thought.

- Are you willing to create and discover the meaning of your life?
- Are you willing to continue to participate in that discovery, that creative process?
- Are you willing to unconditionally accept whatever you dis-cover, whatever you create?

·2·

What's Wrong with Self-Improvement?

Each person's only hope for improving his lot rests on his recognizing the true nature of his basic personality, surrendering to it, and becoming who he is.

SHELDON KOPP

ELF-IMPROVEMENT, the growth industry of the seventies, purported to improve the quality of individuals' lives in the United States. Recovery, the growth industry of the eighties and nineties, seems to promise the same thing.

It's been my experience that much of that recovery, unfortunately, is simply self-improvement repackaged. Self-improvement, by any name, tends to be long on promises and short on effectiveness. Any involvement with a plan or program feels like progress, and the placebo effect of that involvement perpetuates false hope.

More than fifteen million people in this country are currently involved in groups where the focus is on recovery from drug addiction, alcoholism, eating disorders, gambling, destructive relationships, and more. Many others needing help in overcoming these problems, now referred to generically as addictions, are involved in expensive therapy programs often paid for by medical insurance. In addition, millions of Americans continue to invest their time, energy, and money in costly diet, exercise, and image makeover programs. Many businesses serving those people in perpetual quest of self-improvement are now repackaging their programs as recovery.

Recovery Is Not Just a Party Game

The concepts of self-improvement and of recovery have permeated our society. "Tell us something about yourself," Geraldine, the hostess of a recent potluck dinner I attended, encouraged everyone. The responses followed a pattern.

Judith, the graphic artist, began "Hi, I'm Judith, and I'm a recovering compulsive overeater and bulimic."

A gray-haired man smiled and confessed, "I'm a recovering golfer." His wife, playing along, said she was a recovering mother-in-law. A woman in her mid-twenties grinned and admitted that she was a recovering fundamentalist. Her date paused a minute, then said he was recovering from having lousy parents. Cheri was a recovering divorcée.

Harold, on the other hand, was an unrepentant workaholic. Aaron, clearly uncomfortable, remained silent. Katy chimed in with "I'm a recovering chocoholic." Bruce, who had just arrived, said he had a reputation as a procrastinator.

Jane, in an apologetic tone of voice, admitted to being a recovering doormat and people-pleaser. Geraldine concluded by saying she was a recovering compulsive gambler.

Although it became a kind of parlor game, what happened reflects something about the society we live in. At that dinner there were no accountants, no housewives, no business owners, no clerks, just persons "in recovery."

How All This Got Started

The well-established anonymous groups, based on the twelve steps of Alcoholics Anonymous, have enabled millions to begin the process of recovery from life-threatening addictions, difficulties, or traumatic experiences. These Twelve-Step groups, or therapy programs, are often essential for many people in the early stages of recovery from serious problems. Nevertheless, after recovery has begun, after the substance abuse or compulsive behavior is under some control, the individual's life often continues to revolve indefinitely around the concept of addiction.

Avoidance of addictive substances keeps the focus on addiction, and individuals can become overly dependent on the program or group. People with addiction problems who tend to feel alienated from their families and ostracized by society often spend most of their time with others in recovery. Although the power of feeling understood by others is irresistible and the idea that the addict is different or special is validated, both have little to do with true change. When individuals become too attached to these groups, even useful programs and groups can cease to be helpful and become another dependency. If continuing recovery is dependent on something or somebody outside the self, this recovery is vulnerable at best.

Giving your power away to programs, support groups, or other people often creates new problems. Self-improvement newly disguised as recovery often results in unrealistic expectations or overdependency. In addition, some therapy groups or recovery programs can turn into rigid belief systems and dogmatic precepts, both bypassing personal responsibility. Trading dependency on a substance or behavior for a dependency on therapy or a support group may be useful in the beginning, but long-term dependency of any kind is not healthy.

The Role of a Support Group

The role of a support group, program, or therapy early in recovery is to provide information and encouragement during a time of transition and learning. Like a healthy family, the group provides a safe place in which to grow. Later the program or group can function like a halfway house, preparing the person to return to society with constructive habits and attitudes.

Involvement with a group provides a basis for comparing personal problems, stories, and experiences with others. It also serves as a point of reference for those with limited experience and for those who grew up in dysfunctional families and do not know what normal behavior is. The leader or therapist, like a good parent, provides guidelines and models for appropriate behavior as well as honest feedback.

A useful and necessary reliance on the group, however, can become a dependency or an addiction. There's a difference between surrendering oneself to a program of recovery and abandoning oneself to the opinions, definitions, and whims of fellow recoverers. Most good programs like the Twelve-Step programs say, "Take what you like and leave the rest," encouraging people to evaluate continuing participation.

According to many enlightened professionals, if, after two or three years in any therapy or program, all you're doing is going through the motions of attending meetings and your quality of life is still poor, your participation may have become just another habit. Presumably that habit is more positive than the problem it replaced, but true recovery needs to go beyond habit. If living responsibly and sanely and creatively and happily is what you're doing, then going to meetings can be a useful part of your life.

Often it's suggested that newcomers to Twelve-Step programs attend ninety meetings in ninety days as a way of unhooking from an unhealthy life-style. That can be a useful suggestion. However, others who have been in recovery for years have begun to hop back on the ninety-meeting bandwagon. For the recovering person who is working a functional program, perhaps a better challenge may be to make no changes at all for ninety days. This suggestion may sound like heresy to program addicts, but the principle behind it is sound: a commitment to no changes usually increases awareness and conscious involvement that, paradoxically, opens the door to true change. When you stop resisting being lonely, for instance, that feeling will change to anger, or boredom, or something else.

Eventually, it is important to move beyond identifying yourself only in terms of recovery. The old relationship to the group or program that has functioned like a family must eventually be left behind. Make the creation of a new relationship with that family a high priority. Volunteering or becoming a professional working with others in recovery is one way of creating a new relationship with the former family.

A Personal Self-Improvement Odyssey

As a participant over the years in many groups and programs, I am now convinced that good short-term therapy and Twelve-Step groups for people in early recovery are beneficial. However, there comes a time when we need to stop trying to fix ourselves and start accepting our many imperfect selves, to begin living as fully as we can. The aim of recovery or therapy, after all, is to live a full, rich life.

For me, part of that life is my work. As a writer, ideas, words, and language excite me. As a teacher, profound respect for the individual learner challenges me. My passion as a human being is communication; not the one-way act of lecturing, which I also do professionally, but the back-and-forth act of dialogue.

"You really listen," one woman told me after a workshop. I do seek to listen, not only with respect for the individual, but also with attention to more than the words. I don't always succeed. Sometimes my need to jump in with a comment or good advice interferes, and the potential for real communication is short-circuited. Once, after I'd interrupted him for the third time, my friend Aaron gently reminded me, "People need to finish their sentences." Dialogue begins with listening not just with my ears, but with my experience, my intuition, my body, my whole being. "True listening," Aaron also observed, "is hearing someone make a mistake and not correcting them."

I used to care much more about correcting or improving myself and others than being loving and affirming. Years ago when I was a full-time mother, I was determined not only to fix myself, but also to improve my family—for their own good, of course. But my constant attempts to manipulate them created only resentment. Not only did I want things my way, but also I wanted my family to be happy about that.

Now I understand that the least useful thing I can do for those I love is to save them from their own pain. When I try to rescue or protect them from the full realization of their own truths or solve their problems for them, I weaken their initiative and confidence. When they are allowed to make their own mistakes, they learn valuable lessons.

One lesson I've learned is that if I truly love someone, I support that person in bearing the pain of being fallible and of being human. That's the hardest thing to do, to love my friends and family the way they are and to silently support them as they learn from their mistakes. Those learning experiences, the things we call mistakes, result in self-knowledge for them, if I don't interfere.

It has taken me almost thirty years to learn that bit of wisdom. I learned to listen to my inner wisdom as it emerged from my writing, which includes keeping an extensive personal journal. Until recently, however, I figured that everyone else knew more about who I should be, what I should be doing, and how I should be doing it than I did. As I began to fully appreciate the power of my experience and defer less to the opinions of others, I came to realize that I've graduated from the school of hard knocks with the equivalent of a Ph.D. in overcoming guilt, resentment, and self-pity.

When I joined Overeaters Anonymous I paid only lip service to the idea that my problem was not food or weight, but the thoughts and feelings behind the behavior. With the support and encouragement of OA, I lost eighty pounds in nine months, but at that time I didn't recognize that my new behavior was just as compulsive as my eating behavior, and my new obsession to maintain my weight loss at any cost created new problems.

Without extra food to numb my feelings, I became increasingly miserable in my marriage and irrationally felt that I had to choose between regaining the lost weight or divorcing my husband of eighteen years. I chose divorce. After the divorce I became compulsive about buying new clothes and going dancing three nights a week. I seemed to be experiencing a delayed adolescence. In my frenzy to make up for lost time, and preoccupied by the ongoing crises of my life, I continued to neglect my four children and my health. The trouble with burning the candle at both ends was that I ran out of wick.

When a close friend in the OA program killed himself with a pint of whiskey and a bullet to the brain, I tried to console his widow and three children. Although grief-stricken, I couldn't console myself. I was fearful that if my friend hadn't been able to make it, I might not be able to, either.

Since then the purpose of my life has not been just surviving. My daily challenge has become how to help myself to creativity, joy, and well-being. In the process of meeting these daily challenges, I've created a satisfying professional life by passing these techniques along to individuals in my classes, groups, and workshops as well as in the articles and books I write.

A Challenge for You

The ideas and challenges embodied in this book are extended primarily to those who are beyond the initial stages of recovery from serious addictions. They are not a substitute for detox programs, therapy, or medical attention; many conditions, such as obsessive-compulsive disorders, are now possible to treat medically. In addition, if you're currently involved in any group or therapy that is truly having a positive effect, one that isn't just another form of denial or an activity-addiction, don't quit. If your program works, don't fix it.

However, if your problems create serious life complications, consult a professional therapist. Good therapists know that true recovery requires profound changes in perceptions, beliefs, and actions. Good therapists know that self-improvement in search of perfection is a prescription for unhappiness. To improve yourself or give up the addictive substance or behavior without other changes not only can be grim, but it can be dangerous.

The alternative to self-improvement is to develop a creative and life-affirming approach to the whole idea of change and the nature of relationships, especially the most important one, your relationship with yourself. The creative process, in particular, plays a key role in healing and true recovery.

The whole point of recovery or self-improvement is to increase one's quality of life. The following Creative Process can help you evaluate your quality of life or current program. Whether or not you choose to do it now is optional, of course, but it may be useful to take a few minutes to play with it or to mentally note what you may do with it if only you had more time. A playful attitude and a cheerful curiosity will produce optimum results.

Creative Process #2
Duty or Delight?

What is your present quality of life? Here's an easy and interesting way to look at it.

1. Take a sheet of paper and, without thinking about it too much, list your daily Monday through Friday activities. This may include fixing breakfast, commuting to work, working at the computer, doing household chores, eating meals, watching television, playing golf, sewing, talking to friends, exercising or worrying about not exercising. Try to

account for your waking hours—sixteen of the daily twenty-four hours.

2. Using the following grid, developed by psychologist John Enright of Larkspur, California, take each item on your list and place it in the appropriate section—A, B, C, or D. The quadrant where something belongs is dependent on your quality of involvement with it. Washing dishes, for instance, could fit in either of the upper quadrants; some people do them dutifully; there are others who actually enjoy having their hands in hot soapy water. Watching television or reading could fit in section D if you experience doing it as a passive time waster. Or it could belong in either of the upper quadrants depending on whether you experience your involvement as an active and difficult pursuit of knowledge or an active pleasure.

	WANTING TO	NOT WANTING TO
DOING		
	A	B
NOT DOING	D	C

3. *Quadrant D*—Let's start with the lower quadrant on the left side of the grid. Here is where you experience wanting to do or have something, but you are not doing anything to make it happen. This is the home of dreams, daydreams, goals, and fantasies. The time spent here is vaguely enjoyable in a passive kind of way: watching love stories on tele-

vision, for example, instead of socializing; dreaming about winning a marathon instead of jogging. This quadrant, however, can be a breeding ground for frustration when fantasies conflict with daily realities. Items listed here usually represent an energy drain.

Quadrant C—The lower quadrant on the right, also passive, is where duty and moral obligation cohabit and give birth to the guilt and the "shoulds" that make our lives miserable. Procrastination is one of the words describing behavior that fits here. For example: the time spent worrying, fretting, feeling guilty about not-doing, about those undone tasks or other sins of omission such as "I should quit smoking" or "I should answer my mother's letter." Fear, anxiety, and obsession hide here and use the passive energy for their terrorist attacks. How much time do you spend thinking about what you should be doing? How much time do you spend feeling guilty or angry with yourself?

Quadrant B—In the right upper quadrant lies a combat zone where duty feels like drudgery and compulsion lies in ambush, where actions are undertaken because we feel compelled to do them. "I have to wash the dishes after every meal." Anything you don't enjoy, but actually do, no matter how grudgingly, belongs here. For many people ninety percent of their on-the-job time falls in this section.

Quadrant A—The left upper quadrant is where delight and joy and the satisfaction of accomplishment reside. This section is not reserved just for special events. It's for the daily jobs you enjoy: cooking, gardening, practicing the piano, doing the laundry, putting in a good morning's work. Playwright James Barrie once said, "Nothing is work, unless you'd rather be doing something else." Anything you do with wholehearted interest and participation belongs in this area.

Because recovery is undertaken in the first place to increase one's quality of life, one of the hallmarks of true recovery is the transfer of much time and energy from the other three quadrants to Quadrant A, where delight resides. That's where constructive desires lead to action and enjoyment of the process. Small movements, small changes, however, can be as effective in increasing enjoyment as more dramatic gestures. For instance, if worry about not writing to your mother is sapping your energy, hiring someone to write to her could be a way of making three people happier: your mother, yourself, and the person you pay to do it.

In fact, just the act of doing Creative Process #2 will increase your awareness and result in creative problem solving and enhanced enjoyment. Paying attention to potential problem areas can initiate subtle changes, although sometimes it's hard to know when a bad habit may be an early symptom of a serious addiction.

When Too Much Is Not Enough

One sure sign of trouble is when too much is not enough, when there is no such thing as satisfaction. For the alcoholic, one drink is too much and a thousand not enough; for the compulsive overeater, one potato chip is too much because "you can't eat just one"; for the sex addict, one monogamous relationship is too much and a dozen lovers do not satisfy.

Other difficulties can arise when being perfect is the only acceptable standard, when your peace of mind comes from knowing you have a steady supply of your mood-altering substance-of-choice, when life isn't worth living without him or her, or when you feel as if you're living the life that others want you to live. Problems arise when your morning-after hangovers, remorse, and empty promises to reform happen more and more frequently, when being right is more important than being happy, when work-related problems cause you to neglect friends and family, or when you can't say no.

Your quality of life diminishes when watching television becomes more important than doing something creative, when resentment, blame, and self-pity threaten to overwhelm you, or when the people at a party are less important to you than the food or drink being served.

Serious problems are foreshadowed when your pursuit of self-improvement is a cover-up for feelings of inadequacy or loneliness, when you experience no satisfaction from long-term involvement with your therapy or recovery group, or when you've tried and tried to fix yourself and it never works for very long.

Unfortunately, many self-improvement programs tend to emphasize only the problems and their origins and ignore the enjoyment and satisfaction that come from creative solutions to those problems. Beyond self-improvement lies self-esteem and spontaneity, where the focus shifts from the problem to the everyday pleasures of living a balanced life.

Keeping a Daily Journal

For me, living a balanced life means recording things in my current journal, a spiral notebook with a turquoise cover. Everything gets written down carefully, especially when things get really tough, so I know at all times where I am, where I've been, where I'm going, and where I want to go. Then I can sort out the things I can talk out with a friend and what problems I need to take to my therapist.

Both writing and talking about problems work, and they work in somewhat the same way. They are ways of getting problems outside yourself, a way of discharging some of the feelings about your problems, a way to gain perspective. But the act of writing isn't really the most important part. The act of communication itself, expressing thoughts and feelings and being listened to with respect, is the vital component. Writing is an act of communication; the stream-of-consciousness writing of diaries or journals, for instance, is a way of communicating with yourself, of speaking for your moods.

If the idea of that kind of personal writing is anxiety-producing for you, talking into a tape recorder can serve much the same purpose. For most of the Creative Processes suggested in this book, either method can be effective. You don't need previous experience to use a notebook and pen, tape recorder, typewriter, computer—whatever makes you comfortable. (If you choose a typewriter or computer, avoid the temptation to reread or correct typos as you go!)

If you tend to learn best with a hands-on method or through reading, then perhaps writing may be the best way to begin. If you learn best through talking or listening, then starting out with a cassette recorder may be better. These techniques are simple ways of getting a bit of extra information from your subconscious.

Whichever method you choose, protecting the privacy of these writings or recordings is essential. The Creative Processes are designed to be self-revealing. Give yourself permission to destroy them afterwards if that's the only way you can feel safe enough to do them. The important part is doing the Creative Processes: finding out how you got to be the way you are, getting your thoughts and feelings out where you can see or hear them, claiming them as your own, and accepting and releasing them.

The Things That Control Your Life

After all, it's the things we don't know about ourselves that control our lives. Therefore, the more we bring into conscious awareness, the more choice, personal power, and freedom we enjoy.

If you are willing to bring an open mind and a healthy skepticism to the rest of the ideas presented here, you will be able to resist any inclination to give your power away to me. You are encouraged to challenge and even to disagree. There's no one path suitable for everyone. Try these ideas for yourself; discard the ones that don't fit. The hope is that you will find at least two or three good ideas or processes in this book that will make a difference in your life. However, you are the expert on what is useful for you—the important ideas are the ones you prove for yourself.

It's the things we don't know about ourselves
that control our lives.

The ideas in this book are compatible with the principles of most responsible support programs as well as many current therapies. No familiarity with any program or psychological theory is necessary to understand and benefit from these ideas, nor is any religious or spiritual belief required. The ideas and Creative Processes in this book can transform your life—but only if you put them into action. Try out the ones that intrigue you the most.

Food for Thought

The following questions are designed to echo the ideas of this section. You may find your reactions to them more interesting than the questions themselves, especially if you don't take them too seriously. There are no right answers anyway.

• Do you understand and respect your basic personality?
• Are you willing to surrender to your true nature?
• Are you hooked on improving yourself, or are you engaged in the process of becoming who you are?
• Is it possible that all that is wrong with you may be other people's opinions?

· 3 ·

True Recovery Doesn't Have White Knuckles

*I have used all my doubt as energy, and created with
it. I have used all my pain as energy, and created with
it. I have used all my anxiety as energy, and created
with it. I plan to use my death as energy, and create
with it, no matter what Death's plans are for me.*

STYMEAN KARLEN

TRUE RECOVERY often begins as a positive goal or a
dream of something better. When that goal is freely
chosen and is coupled with action, true change can occur. Although negative techniques do not usually produce true
recovery or real change, using the negative energy of doubt,
pain, and fear as a creative force can provide a positive focus
for recovery from addiction.

Most addictions are attempts to control pain, to control the
uncertainty of life, or to avoid solving problems. Freedom
from pain, freedom from uncertainty, freedom from having to
face problems is the unconscious goal. Addictions seem to
provide a temporary time-out from difficult or painful events,
disappointments, or circumstances.

Unfortunately, addictions bring a different set of painful
consequences and also provide a scapegoat that masks the real

problem. "It's not my fault, it's the alcohol that's the problem."
"I just can't resist chocolate." "If I want to be successful I have
to work seven days a week." "I need love." "It's the refrigerator
calling to me." "The credit card companies make it too easy
for me to buy things I don't need." "If the cocaine is there, I
gotta do it." "But, he's good to me when he's not drinking."

And addicts, even in recovery, can blame the substance or
the focus of the behavior and avoid the pain of responsibility
for their lives. When we blame something or someone else for
what happens to us, we are ducking accountability. When we
hold others responsible for our emotions, our thoughts, our
feelings, we perpetuate irresponsibility and delay any possible
recovery.

Many people, however, are motivated to change, to improve, or to strive for recovery by a sense of duty or dependence on the opinion or approval of others. When people
cling to a group with grim determination—with white
knuckles—any change is short-lived at best. When people say
it's the therapist or the support group that is responsible for
their recovery, or when they stay in a program for fear of relapse, their quality of life remains poor.

Desperate and unhappy reasons bring people to therapy or
support programs. "I was afraid I was going to die." "My wife
said I was killing myself and she was leaving me." "I often
wished I were dead." "My brother said he'd kill me if I didn't
quit." People who attend Twelve-Step programs speak of "getting sick and tired of feeling sick and tired." This negative re-
inforcement can initiate change, but unless there is an eventual
shift to a positive goal, true change and satisfaction remain out
of reach.

Fred's Story

Fred, the alcoholic carpenter, became sober at the age of forty
because "my family told me how much my drinking was hurt-

ing them. So I got on the wagon and stopped drinking; I went to AA and got with the program."

In the beginning Fred received a lot of support and attention from his family and friends. Then they began feeling resentful because he still was not what they wanted him to be. His wife complained, "You're gone all the time." Fred was attending three AA meetings and one group therapy session every week. "You're not as nice as you used to be," his best friend commented. The ways in which Fred was changing and his growing honesty made others feel uncomfortable.

When people are involved in destructive addictive behavior, such as drinking, gambling, overspending, suicide attempts, bulimic purging, or abusive relationships, they often get the message that everything will be okay if only they don't do *that*—whatever *that* is—anymore. In the early stages of recovery they begin to feel better, their self-esteem rises, and their quality of life improves. Their relationships, however, often suffer.

At first Fred felt lucky because he had learned that addiction is a family disease, and his family started getting help, too. His wife joined AlAnon, his children attended AlaTeen. Then everybody in the family was gone all the time, and they were not as "nice" as they used to be. Conflict between Fred and his wife escalated; when one person in a relationship changes, it creates a change in the family dynamics.

Even the most dysfunctional family has familiar patterns "Watch out for Dad when he's drunk." When Dad no longer drinks, the family doesn't know what to expect and feels uneasy. Dad responds to this uneasiness with withdrawal or anger. When familiar family patterns are disrupted by one person's recovery, it can seem more difficult to create new ways of relating than it would be to make more drastic changes.

Fred became more and more involved with his support groups. Eventually he divorced and cut himself off from all former relationships. Although change does happen to people in therapy or in recovery, it is not predictable.

Family Involvement in Recovery

People in recovery are people involved with unpredictable change. Therefore, families and friends of those in recovery are also affected by unpredictable change. If you are reading this book because of concern for someone who has a problem, and you want to learn more about what he or she is going through, the best thing you can do to help is to use this information to upgrade the quality of your own life. The suggested Creative Processes in each chapter will positively benefit anyone who is willing to spend the time and energy to do them.

Some of you may be reading this because you have a relationship, or a problem, with someone in recovery or with someone you think should be in therapy. It's important to shift your focus where it belongs: onto yourself. You may not experience needing to recover from addiction, or illness, or divorce, or other life-changing event. Chances are, however, that you may need to recover from something, even if it is just your need to see a loved one change in a certain way. Although it is not possible for those who have not lived through the same problems to fully understand what a person in recovery must go through, doing these Creative Processes will help you to appreciate how difficult and scary it can sometimes be to learn about oneself.

Often the person who loves someone with a problem needs to recover from the doubt, fear, hurt, resentment, and blame that that relationship seems to have created. Sometimes the person needs to recover from moral superiority or righteousness. Fred's wife, for instance, needed to recover from her need to control and manipulate Fred, which not only slowed his progress but also interfered with good communication.

If you have a problem with someone in recovery, work on your thoughts and feelings about that person. Your problem is how to deal with your opinions and judgments of that person's behavior, decisions, actions, and words. People in trouble cannot be helped by someone trying to rescue them from the pain of confronting themselves. We all must be allowed to have our own feelings and to face the consequences of our behavior.

Recovery Requires a Death

Reinhold Niebuhr wrote, "The conquest of self is in a sense the inevitable consequence of true self-knowledge. If the self-centered self is shattered by a genuine awareness of its situation, there is the power of a new life in the experience." The new life reflected in true recovery requires profound change, the kind of change that often feels like a death of sorts—the death of an unhealthy life-style, not merely a change in behavior; the death of a false belief system, not just showing up for therapy. Facing these deaths, these losses, is painful.

Most people become open to changing, to therapy, or to support programs only when the daily pain of living with the problem becomes greater than the feared pain of dealing with the problem. However, if recovery is not accompanied by profound changes not only in one's behavior, relationships, or environment, but also in one's fundamental relationship with oneself, then suicide can seem like the best choice.

Relapse is a less drastic option. The individual returns to the living death of substance abuse or addictive behavior. As persons in an addictive society, we instinctively understand and fear the pain of the death of our lives as we have known them. Addictive persons often deny their own reality, resist profound change, and perpetuate their negative and addictive systems.

Society Sends Conflicting Messages

Our society creates confusion and reinforces denial of reality through patterns of conspicuous consumption and out-of-control debt while it preaches restraint. Madison Avenue sends mixed messages by encouraging overeating and alcoholic good times while teaching "You can't be too rich or too thin," which fosters compulsive spending and eating disorders. Looking good is more important than being happy or healthy.

The lust for a perfect body increases the use of steroids, liposuction, and cosmetic surgery. Other minor addictions such as caffeine, chocolate, cigarettes, credit card debt, and television—Saturday morning cartoons, Monday night football, soap operas—are taken for granted as a normal part of American life.

Workaholism and perfectionism are disguised as excellence. Organized sports, from Little League to the Olympics, encourage sportsmanship, but focus more on corporate sponsors and winning at any cost. Romantic love, marriage, and the family are supposed to reflect American values; popular magazines and television talk shows, addicted to sensationalism, polarize the sexes by celebrating infidelity, divorce, and the negative aspects of relationships.

Even the best support programs often unwittingly perpetuate a negative focus by reinforcing fear of the abused substance or behavior, fear of relapse, fear of further loss. That's why the people who often do best in these programs are those who have nothing left to lose. When a person has already alienated friends and family, can't hold a job, or is perpetually in trouble, that individual is more likely to stay with a program of recovery that promises a way out.

Debbie's Story

Debbie, a twenty-eight-year-old cocktail waitress who was newly married, had plenty to lose when she finally admitted that she was an alcoholic. In previous years she had been involved with both drugs and alcohol. Her former boyfriend was an alcoholic whose best friend was a cocaine dealer. She had worked in an industry fueled by alcohol and drugs. She had painfully extricated herself from that relationship, had given up drugs, and had cut down on alcohol use.

During times of sobriety and remorse she'd been reminded that alcoholism is a physical disease, a progressive disease, and that her mother's side of the family exhibited an intolerance for alcohol. She had long resisted the idea that she couldn't handle controlled drinking.

Debbie attended some AA meetings and realized the necessity of making some changes, including getting out of the restaurant business. Young and physically healthy, she proved she could stop drinking for short periods of time, so maintaining abstinence from alcohol long enough to recover physically wasn't the problem. Debbie's challenge was to engage in the process of recovery from the mental, emotional, and spiritual effects of the disease called alcoholism.

The recovery process consists of some important principles. Groups modeled on AA follow twelve steps, and other therapy programs talk about the process of recovery in different ways. But the principles of recovery seem consistent:

- To accept that you have a problem
- To seek recovery for yourself, not for anyone else
- To have the vision of a better life beyond recovery
- To find the courage to change your life-style and beliefs
- To ask for and accept help
- To work at daily self-examination
- To seek your true character
- To understand and embrace your past
- To find a higher purpose for your life

Debbie had already begun the first parts of that process: "I know I'm an alcoholic, because when I take even one drink I don't know where it will stop anymore. I want to stop drinking for myself. I feel I can accomplish great things if I'm sober, and I'm willing to quit my job as a cocktail waitress. I'm going to find people who can help me through this." Debbie understood the other requirements for recovery and was prepared to do whatever it took—not only to remain sober, but also to create a meaningful life for herself.

Basic necessities that aid in any recovery process are awareness and responsibility. With awareness and responsibility some people take charge of their own recovery in unorthodox ways. Hannah, for instance, when abruptly widowed, refused the prescribed tranquilizers and moved to the wilderness to live in a tent on a riverbank for a year and a half while she healed from her loss. Her happy depression-era childhood had taken place in just such an environment.

Elaina, an office manager, was recovering from an abusive relationship and its consequent terrors. She realized that the management career that enabled her to afford therapy was making her sicker. So, over the protests of her family, she got a job as a part-time sales clerk, moved into a tiny rented room, and began "wandering." For six to eight hours a day, rain or shine, she rambled around the city thinking things over, writing things down, and mastering her fears. Two years later she felt well enough to return to full-time work and renewed participation in family life.

Aaron, suffering job burnout, quit a stressful job in the insurance field and for three years built a twenty-foot wooden sailboat and created many fanciful rocking animals including Smoky, an adult-sized green dragon. Although he eventually returned to the same occupation, he did so with increased confidence and a sense of what was really important in his life.

The Need for Professional Help

Conscious recovery is more difficult for those who are caught in addictive or compulsive cycles where denial is a primary symptom. Addictions and compulsions feed on unconscious patterns or habits of thinking and behavior. Therefore, people suffering from these kinds of problems may need professional help. Many addicts do not remember, or want to remember, what they have done, much less experience the moment when they chose the thought or action. The addiction dulls awareness; blame and denial invalidate personal responsibility; accountability is bypassed.

Denial is a fundamental symptom of any addiction. That's why many programs for addicts begin with a system for documenting what's happening. For instance, awareness of overspending is increased when a written record of every purchase is kept. It also results in greater accountability. Awareness of obsessive thinking patterns can be heightened by a daily tally of how often a particular thought occurs. Because we can be responsible only for that which we can control, and then only to the extent to which we have control, collecting the facts is an important early step.

Increased awareness is the first step to change, which can lead to experiencing choice and taking responsibility for thoughts and actions. "I had no choice" and "There was nothing else I could do" are evasions of responsibility.

Increased awareness, however, often feels overwhelming, and the successes that friends and relatives celebrate soon begin to make them feel uncomfortable. "Fred's so pure now that he makes me look bad," complained his brother. That's why people in the early stages of recovery, alienated from their families and ostracized by society, often spend most of their time with others in recovery.

The shared preoccupation with addiction gives individuals a continued sense of separateness from the community. In therapy programs and support groups, however, they find people struggling with the same problems as well as their own sense of belonging, which can be useful at first. Substituting the former addiction for dependence on the group often is a necessary and positive step during the early years of a good recovery.

The Pain of Addiction

Awareness can be painful, conscious choice can be painful, and responsibility can be painful, especially if we take life very seriously. Conscious participation in therapy or support groups helps us experience the results of our choices. The extent to which we can accept the consequences of our choices is the extent to which we are being responsible.

Harold, a successful business executive in his mid-fifties, often complained, "I'm living the life others want me to live." Although he was a forceful and dynamic business leader, he felt no ability to control his personal life. His unconscious solution was to become a workaholic who had no time for himself and his family. He did the things that duty demanded; as the oldest son and head of the family business, he took care of his elderly mother and his alcoholic brother.

Harold knew his brother needed help. He never considered, however, that his own workaholism might be a problem, because he provided a good living for his wife and children and fair benefits for his employees. He felt righteous, resigned, and trapped. He also felt lonely and unappreciated, and he often dreamed of joining the Peace Corps. Even his dream included taking care of others.

Harold escaped facing the pain of his choices and responsibility for his happiness by blaming others. His addiction to blaming others masked the personal pain that may have encouraged him to seek help for himself.

Wanting to avoid the pain of addictive behavior brings many people to support programs, but avoiding pain isn't true recovery. Freedom is the proper goal for true recovery: freedom from anxiety, freedom from helplessness, freedom from perfectionism, freedom from overdependence.

Freedom to make decisions and mistakes is necessary for the development of responsibility. The natural consequences of our choices are the best lessons in decision making and responsibility.

Negative-Based Recovery Is Doomed

True recovery begins when the person finds something creative—something positive to do, to be, to aim for. Sarah, a full-time homemaker, on the other hand, always knew what she *didn't* want: "I don't want to be anything like my mother." She saw her mother as vain and shallow, unmotherly and irresponsible. Sarah's mother was slender and vivacious; she loved new clothes and lots of attention; she had the gift of gab and little interest in food. She was also often ill and bedridden.

Sarah became ultra-responsible; she began cooking and keeping house for her mother and younger brothers at the age of nine, developed a weight problem, and disdained fashion and frivolity. Like many children from dysfunctional families, she missed some important growth steps: safety, trust, intimacy, and self-expression. Sarah married young and began having babies immediately, determined to raise her children with the love and devotion she felt she'd missed. However, her need to control her husband and children and, therefore, her circumstances, led to frustration, despair, and serious compulsive overeating.

Ten years later Sarah emerged from an eating binge twenty pounds heavier than she'd ever been before. She was obsessed because, although she was barely more than five feet tall, she weighed as much as Joe Namath did. Once again she knew what she didn't want. She knew she didn't want to be heavier. She was tired of constantly thinking about food. She was tired of feeling guilty for eating too much, too often, and for the wrong reasons. She was afraid of getting fatter.

Freedom is the proper goal for true recovery.

Sarah began a stringent diet. She began to lose weight, but she often felt frantic and deprived. She had switched from obsessive thinking about eating to obsessive focus on not-eating, from fear of hunger and emptiness to fear of food and fatness. She was told, "Don't even think of taking that first bite"; therefore, she was always thinking about that first bite. (If I say to you, "Don't think of a pink elephant," what do you think of?) Her weight fluctuated for years and so did her quality of life, because her self-esteem was dependent on the numbers on her bathroom scale.

Another case of negative-based recovery was happy-go-lucky Neil, a salesman who hadn't planned on marriage, but his girlfriend's pregnancy and parental pressure turned him into a family man. Alcohol, which helped him avoid the pain of a life he felt he hadn't chosen, led him into alcoholism, which created different kinds of pain: drunken outbursts, guilt, blackouts, remorse. And it was the pain of his family and their nagging that brought him into the support groups that helped him stay sober. At last there was no escape, no time-out from the pain of being Neil. In the eyes of his family and the world, he had changed. He had changed his behavior; he was behaving in a more responsible way.

Neil, however, unlike Harold, didn't feel responsible; he felt resentful and trapped. The changes he'd made were under-taken for his family and didn't really satisfy him. He wanted to quit his job, which often took him into taverns and bars; he wanted to move to a small town and grow his own vegetables; he wanted to be a hunting guide. His family did not want to move or change its standard of living. Neil, dependent on family approval and no longer able to drown his sorrows, saw no other way out. He killed himself. If Neil had been willing to act in his own behalf and separate from his family, he may not have ended up abandoning them in a much more devastating way.

Negative-based recovery like Sarah's is short-lived. Duty-based recovery like Neil's is doomed. Most efforts to teach responsibility succeed mostly in teaching blame, resentment, and irresponsibility. True recovery is characterized by a freedom of expression, a freedom from fear and guilt; not only freedom from obsession, compulsion, and the need to control others, but also freedom from being vulnerable to control by others. Freedom is the ability to experience choice—the widest possible range of behavior options. Freedom means accepting responsibility without resentment.

If you feel caught in the inertia that keeps company with self-pity and resentment, the following plan can provide a beginning toward autonomy and responsibility. If you're feeling stuck in therapy or a support group, these ideas can invigorate your participation. If you're already involved in a plan of recovery that is working for you, use the next Creative Process as a way of measuring the effectiveness of your program.

Many Creative Processes in this book can help you keep a sense of perspective during the process of recovering creativity, joy, and well-being. One way to gain perspective is to make sure some time each day is spent in active enjoyment of the little things, the "petite happinesses."

Creative Process #3
Antidote to Inertia

Sometimes it's hard to break out of habits of passivity and nonaction. Stuck in the familiarity of the status quo, we remain paralyzed by inertia. It's often been said that it takes twenty-one days to build a new habit, so here are some suggested ideas to try daily for three weeks. I don't know whether you're going to agree with this process or merely accept the ideas and concepts. And that's not what's important. What is important is that you feel good about what you believe. That makes sense, doesn't it?

This four-part antidote to inertia is simple enough for anyone to use or adapt for individual needs. Although the suggestions may sound simplistic, they often produce interesting and beneficial results. Perhaps you're already doing some of them. The immediate goal is to work up to a minimum of two hours each day spent in any of the following ways:

1. Brisk walking, dancing, gardening, or other enjoyable physical activity
2. Communicating thoughts and feelings
3. People contacts: in-person or telephone
4. Involvement in any creative endeavor: drawing, painting, or photography; knitting, woodworking, pottery, or other

craft; writing poems, stories, or songs; singing or playing a musical instrument just for fun

Start with the areas that you are currently not active in. Devote twenty minutes daily to them. For instance, if you're physically inactive or handicapped, walking around the block twice a day or dancing to your favorite song for a few minutes in your living room may be a great beginning. If you're sports minded, avoid the kinds of physical sports or games that involve score-keeping. This is about involvement, not performance.

It's especially useful to be outdoors. Depending on your location and the time of year, indulge in some leaf-kicking, snow-crunching, kite-flying, surf-dancing, flower-sniffing, puddle-wading activities. Every spring, for example, I make a pilgrimage to the glorious old pink dogwood tree on a nearby college campus. The blossoms, like a cloud of hovering pink butterflies, never fail to lift my spirits.

If communicating thoughts and feelings is out of your comfort zone, writing a letter or jotting down ideas may be a useful stretch. Recording little pleasures in a daily journal can increase awareness and appreciation of the simple joys. A journal or diary can function like a portable friend—always available, always ready to listen. Give your journal a friendly name; Frank is a great name for a journal, or Joy.

If you are shy or uncomfortable around people, begin by talking to store clerks or going to a meeting or discussion group where you'll be encouraged to participate. Or, compliment your neighbors on their colorful seasonal flower displays.

There's a difference between being a happy introvert who prefers small groups of people and enjoys productive solitude, and the unhappy or painful isolation from which many individuals are trying to emerge. The right balance between time with others and time alone may take a while to establish.

Creative involvement means doing anything in which you take pleasure and tend to lose track of time. There may be some overlap among the four areas; writing a poem or a letter may be both creative and a way of communicating feelings; woodworking or pottery making or dancing or gardening may be both physical and creative; having a heart-to-heart discussion with a friend combines communicating feelings with people contact.

Find an easy way to keep track of what you do each day; if you don't currently keep a journal, simply noting accomplishments on the squares of a calendar may be enough.

The Value of Creativity

The more creativity you experience, the more your quality of life will improve. Eventually your creative attitude will provide more interesting options, not only for dealing with problems but also with ordinary tasks.

Not too long ago I made out my will; I'd been putting it off for years because it seemed like a depressing and morbid thing to do. A friend finally talked me into it and suggested a lawyer.

As I began to tell the lawyer how I wanted things handled, I found it gave me an opportunity to express my values. I wanted no extreme measures taken to keep me alive, so I made a living will, and I also requested cremation.

Then I began worrying about my ashes; I didn't want them lingering around in an urn. Finally I thought about the forty-foot fishing boat my oldest son, Rick, had built in his front yard and had named the *FV Roberta Jean*. I requested that my ashes be scattered from the stern of the boat into the ocean. It seemed like a creative solution, and the idea delighted me—an expression of my love of the water and my appreciation of freedom.

The rest of my will was pretty straightforward—to divide my estate equally among my four children, Rick, Deborah, Michael, and Ron. However, the idea of reducing it all just to a matter of dollars offended me; I've never been particularly materialistic. So I concluded with a request that they use the money for education or travel.

The experience of drawing up my will was a lot more fun than I had thought it could be because I allowed myself to use the idea of my death to create with. Others who have done the same thing include Elisabeth Kubler-Ross, who writes and teaches about death and dying. Poets, storytellers, songwriters, and blues singers tap into that kind of energy, also. On a more mundane level, hospice workers spend the energy of their mortality to ease the last days of other people.

Food for Thought

Think of these chapters as an offering of ideas from which to pick and choose, like a Chinese buffet. These questions can be viewed as a provocative assortment of fortune cookie messages:

- What are your doubts? Are you using them as energy? Are you creating with them?
- What is your pain? Are you using it as energy? Are you creating with it?
- What are your anxieties? Are you using them as energy? Are you creating with them?
- Are you willing to use your death as energy and start creating with it?

· II ·
Self-Acceptance, Power, and the Past

· 4 ·

True Change:
The Magic of Profound
Self-Acceptance

*Change occurs when you become what you are, not
when you try to become what you are not. . . . Change
seems to happen when you have abandoned the chase
after what you want to be (or think you should be) and
have accepted—and fully experienced—what you are.*

JANETTE RAINWATER

TRUE CHANGE means becoming who you really are in a natural and organic way. Although true change is possible and sometimes happens during therapy or in good recovery programs, it seldom results from self-improvement promises or programs. It occurs in three ways:

1. A near-death or born-again experience
2. Bottoming out—a state of physical, emotional, or spiritual bankruptcy
3. Profound self-acceptance

"There is another way," Aaron protested after hearing me lecture one evening. "When I'm around a person who is loving and nurturing, then I begin to change." His changing, however, was dependent on having someone else for a catalyst, and he admitted that once again he was seeking the kind of person who could provide it.

Examples of this kind of dependent change occur for persons involved in self-improvement groups or programs. That is one way of experiencing profound self-acceptance. However, the changes that happen are the result of "I accept myself, because this person or group that I esteem accepts me." The falling-in-love phenomenon and the therapist-as-guru relationship are two examples of this kind of conditional change.

These routes to change are often less productive, less lasting, and less satisfying than seeking that experience of acceptance within oneself. The dependence on an outside source for a positive sense of self always places our "okayness" and our authenticity at risk. Good therapists do not encourage that kind of dependency, but consistently remind clients that their quality of life is determined by them, not the therapist or well-meaning friends and family.

"When we must deal with problems," observed Carl Jung, "we instinctively refuse to try the way that leads through darkness and obscurity. We wish to hear only of unequivocal results and completely forget that these results can only be brought about when we have ventured into and emerged again from the darkness."

Profound self-acceptance is a search for truth within the darkness of oneself. Albert Schweitzer noted, "Truth has no special time of its own. Its hour is now—always." As a matter of fact, people always tell the truth; even their lies reflect the truth of their secret wishes, hopes, and dreams. Truth, however, is layered, like an onion or an artichoke. So the task of becoming free is akin to peeling away layers of truth, like the leaves of an artichoke, to uncover that core truth that transforms experience.

Profound self-acceptance is a search for the truth, the individual and personal truth of the seeker, not some abstract eternal truth. This ongoing search requires hard work, an investment of time in self-examination, and honesty—honesty with oneself primarily and possibly with a trusted friend, spiritual advisor, or therapist.

In Search of Your Truths

When misery drove me to seek out a psychiatrist early in my marriage, I'm sure I regaled him with an exhaustive list of my shortcomings, character defects, and neuroses. A Freudian therapist, he seldom spoke—maybe one sentence per session—and therefore I remember them all. His smiling comment after that first session was "Well, at least your sins are the warm ones."

I treasured that comment, often reassuring myself that gluttony, sloth, lust, and anger—which I admitted to—were better than pride, envy, and covetousness—which I pridefully thought I was not guilty of. That was the beginning of profound self-acceptance for me—accepting my warm sins. Then came the day when, searching for my own truth, I realized that I envied a friend's success. That admission opened the door to the greater truth: I, like every other human being, was capable of any sin and any feeling. I was not proud of my sins, but I was finally willing to own them, to accept them.

Another milestone in my personal struggle toward accepting myself came a few years ago at a shopping mall. I'd just bought three new diet books, hoping one of them would have the magic words that would change my life and my body. On impulse, I'd also purchased the latest Jane Fonda workout video. My next stop, which I'd been dreading, was to find something to wear for the speech I was to give at the regional PTA council.

In the department store I headed for the sale rack, looking for an inexpensive dark-colored dress to cover up the extra pounds I wanted to magic away. I finally found a navy nylon shirtwaist in a size I used to wear; it was half-price. As I headed to the changing room, a soft, rose-pink wool dress caught my eye; I loved the color and the texture, and I couldn't resist trying it on. The navy dress turned out to be tight, but would be perfect when I lost weight; the rose-pink dress in a larger size fit beautifully and felt wonderful, but it cost three times what the other one did.

"May I help you?" the sales clerk asked as I approached the counter. I held up both dresses and asked her opinion. She eyed my figure and pointed to the navy dress.

"I'll take this one," I said, handing her the rose-pink dress. I felt defiant, delighted, and terrified of spending that much money on my nonperfect self. But with that act I accepted my body just the way it was, accepted my preference for a wonderful color, accepted my right to feel comfortable in my clothes, and affirmed my right to own an expensive dress, no matter what. My next act was to return the books and video I'd purchased earlier. The refund nearly cancelled out the difference in price between the two dresses, and I experienced an enormous sense of relief.

Jane's Story

Jane, an insecure homemaker and mother of two, found it impossible to accept herself. Years earlier, when she was first married, her greatest fear was that if her husband ever found out what she was really like, he wouldn't like her anymore. Therefore, she was also unconsciously afraid of even allowing *herself* to know what she was really like, because if that happened, it could rock the boat.

Her belief that if she discovered something wasn't right she had to do something about it kept her stuck in denial of her unhappy marriage. She unconsciously knew that doing something about it would be too difficult and would jeopardize her family's security. Those fears, conscious and unconscious, were one layer of truth.

Eventually, Jane began to become more honest with herself and to risk sharing that discovered self with her husband. She also spoke up more often and on occasion even contradicted what he said. Sure enough, he complained about her getting "uppity," they began quarreling more frequently, and she felt that he didn't like her—her greatest fear come true. That layer of truth ultimately led to divorce, which did indeed jeopardize her family's security. Soon after her divorce Jane experienced a chaos of emotions, but also discovered a core truth that transformed a major emotional problem in her life.

Jane had emerged from her divorce at the tender age of forty feeling profoundly abandoned by her ex-husband for not liking her and irrationally angry at his refusal to contest the divorce. She was devastated by his plans to remarry. A confusing jumble of resentment and self-pity about her abandonment dominated her waking moments. No matter what else happened to her, those deeply felt obsessive thoughts and feelings overshadowed the rest of her life.

This wasn't the first time she'd felt so hurt and lost.

When Jane was five years old her mother had deserted her father, packing hurriedly and sneaking off one afternoon with Janie and her brother. Janie had not understood what was happening and had no chance to say good-bye to her father. Also, she was never allowed to talk about it. Consequently, a part of her often felt hurt and lost when people did not keep their agreements, and on occasion, when a trusted person let her down, the abandonment feelings overwhelmed and devastated her.

Whenever those feelings were triggered she became, in effect, an adult Jane with five-year-old Janie in the driver's seat; she looked and often acted like a responsible adult, but emotionally the hurt child ruled. Her relationships suffered because other people often became targets of Janie's unprovoked and irrational emotional outbursts. Jane, herself, found it terrifying to be an unpredictable adult with no control over her reactions and feelings. Even understanding the whys of her problem didn't help her to react or feel different. Insight brought no relief, just greater frustration.

The day things changed was the day when she uncovered and accepted the core truth about her abandonment issue.

Jane and her best friend, Tom, whom she thought of as the older brother she'd always wanted, usually shared their problems over lunch in local restaurants. That day, Jane, feeling bereft and lonely, began weeping as she often did in those days following her divorce. "How could he let me divorce him," she wailed, recounting her grievances against her former husband. "And now he's planning to marry her! How dare he abandon me and the children like this?"

Finally Tom reached across the table, touched her hand to get her attention, and said, "Janie, I will never abandon you." That sincere promise from a man she totally trusted stopped her litany of self-pity and resentment. That moment of affirmation and friendship warmed a frozen place within her; she began to feel loved again. At the same instant, though, inside her head a little voice whispered, "But, it's not enough!"

She couldn't believe what was happening. That clear moment when Tom expressed his loyalty to her was rudely interrupted by that invalidating whisper. Then, just to make sure she couldn't ignore it, the little voice repeated, "But, it's not enough."

Later, at home with her journal, Jane attempted to reason with that little voice. "Don't you believe Tom?" she wrote.

"Yes, but it's still not enough." Janie, the abandoned child within her, wouldn't be persuaded. Finally, discouraged by the determined stance of that young part of herself, she remembered how she'd learned to deal with her own children during their temper tantrums—putting her arms around them, saying "There, there, everything's going to be all right." So, Jane began listing all the things she really appreciated about that young part of herself, comforting and consoling Janie without being dishonest.

Finally she wrote, "I will never abandon you." Jane, the grown-up part of her, would not abandon or invalidate the feelings of the Janie part of herself. Jane's core truth was the realization that she could not experience such total devastation unless she also ran out on—abandoned—that hurting child within. At that moment her experience of feeling abandoned profoundly changed and improved her control over her own life. However, she continued to struggle with a festering load of resentment against her former husband and sought relief from that growing obsession. Three years after the divorce, still engaged in her search for truths, she peeled off the final leaf and encountered the heart of the artichoke—the core truth—about her relationship with her former husband.

Core truths always transform experience.

That final leaf was the sudden realization that she was spending so much time reacting to what he had said or had done it was as if she was still married to him. After she'd acknowledged that, the core truth lay revealed. Jane finally discovered what she was really like, and had to admit that she hadn't liked her husband very much. Divorce had been her idea, not his.

Recognizing and accepting her responsibility for all that had happened freed her from the resentment of "Look what he did to me!" Core truths always transform experience, and always have to do with oneself, never with one's upbringing or what anyone else says or does, past or present. Core truths always evolve from profound self-acceptance.

The Four Levels of Profound Self-Acceptance

Profound self-acceptance is not a fixed state of being, but a spiraling evolution of truth and awareness that seems to consist of four levels. During the course of any period of growth, we move up and down the spiral many times, or move from one level to the next, or even back to the previous one.

The first level of profound self-acceptance appears to be negative and may not be experienced by everyone. A person at this level says, "Something is wrong with me. I know I'm not okay." No one can talk the person out of this feeling. "I don't need anybody. Nobody cares anyway. I'm not even worth improving. People don't like me; they won't give me a chance."

The person is passive, depressive, and feels and sounds like a victim: alienated, unconnected, feeling unworthy of human companionship.

These individuals either lack heroes and goals, or their standards for themselves and others are so perfectionistic that they tend to hear only negative feedback or to insist on a gloomy interpretation of all events. But in this stage, the beginning of profound self-acceptance is becoming aware of how nonaccepting one really is, accepting it, and not punishing oneself further for it.

The second level is characterized by what is now being called codependency—in which another person's behavior affects us so intensely that we are obsessed with controlling that other person. On the second level the focus often shifts from knowing something is wrong with me to knowing there's something wrong with you, too, and often evolving to "What's wrong with me is all your fault," or the notion that if *you* get help, then everything will be just fine with *me*.

Moving from the first level to the second level sounds like this at first: "I'm okay, if you tell me I'm okay." The person works hard at self-improvement and at pleasing others to get approval. Sometimes the person tries to "fix" others and thereby gets the illusion of control over people, events, and circumstances.

In another variation the individual moves from self-blame to blaming others: "I'm okay if you're not okay" or "I wouldn't overspend if you only earned enough money" or "I wouldn't drink if you didn't nag me so much" or "I wouldn't nag you so much if you didn't drink." It's a vulnerable and volatile level, however, because the person's worth is dependent on outside reassurance.

Individuals at level two live on an emotional seesaw, seldom in touch with their true feelings, usually operating out of fear—fear of anger or fear of rejection. They often have unrealistic expectations of themselves and others and ignore reality, lie, or manipulate to avoid direct conflict. They overidealize their role models and objects of affection. Addicted to immediate gratification, intensity, and drama—the soap opera of their own lives—they live in a world of denial and fantasy.

Cultivating profound self-acceptance creates awareness; awareness is the opposite of denial; becoming aware and accepting small truths begins to replace denial. Denial diminishes with every accepting thought or statement; an attitude of profound self-acceptance also fosters true responsibility that gradually replaces fantasy.

On the third level individuals say, "I'm okay, even by myself," accepting responsibility for their happiness and solving their problems. They work hard at helping others for their own satisfaction and not just to please others. Active, reality-oriented, and often self-actualizing, they value themselves and others and see former heroes and role models as equals. If no one is any better than I am, if no one is any lesser than I am, if I see all of us as imperfect human beings, then I can be open and learn from all human encounters. This level is where people tend to be goal-oriented.

The fourth level attitude is, "Isn't this interesting!" There's a cheerful curiosity toward possibilities and a willingness to show up and see what will happen today. For these individuals the whole notion of self-improvement is alien; the idea wouldn't even arise. They have an easy acceptance of all events, circumstances, and people. Value judgments of good and bad or right and wrong seldom are made. At this level they remain detached, immune to being influenced by popular opinion—like the best mothers, who, according to Hermann Hesse's *Siddhartha*, "learn not to care; to separate." Open and flexible, happy more often than not, they live fully in the moment with great appreciation of the cosmic humor of the human condition.

Accepting Your Imperfect Self

Whatever level you find yourself at, profound self-acceptance does not require approving of yourself or liking all aspects of yourself; neither does it mean a superficial Pollyannaish counting of blessings. Accepting yourself does not require you to announce the character defects you discover; neither does it entail defiance—"That's just the way I am; take it or leave it!"—or apologizing for what you find. There's no blaming yourself or others, and no explaining or over-explaining.

Profound self-acceptance saves us from the ego trips of the comparison game, the I'm-better-than or holier-than-thou attitudes of arrogance and righteousness, or the lesser-than comparisons resulting in "poor me" or self-pity. The magic in profound self-acceptance is that the more you are willing to know and accept in yourself, the more you know about and accept in other people. As human beings there are more similarities among us than real differences; we all are led or driven by our feelings—our sorrows and joys as well as our assumptions and beliefs about ourselves and others.

Accepting your imperfect self includes accepting:

- The ways you are like your parents
- Any socially inappropriate behavior
- All your thoughts—past, present, and future
- All your feelings
- The physical body you were born with
- Your looks, your height, your weight
- Any relationships that didn't work out
- Your income and social status
- All your faults and character defects
- All the ways you have discounted yourself
- Anything you've ever tried to improve or change about yourself

Profound self-acceptance is sometimes bound to be difficult. To love and accept ourselves unconditionally is no problem when things are going well; it's easy when we get up in the morning, look in the mirror, smile at ourselves, and like what we see. The real challenge is to accept ourselves when we're really messing up. We straggle out of bed; we don't want to look in the mirror; things are definitely not okay. That's when profound self-acceptance is most necessary.

The process of profound self-acceptance is simple, but not necessarily easy. I start by acknowledging the obvious, making a detailed inventory of everything that's going on for me at the present moment. It may sound like I was crabby: "I don't feel like getting up today, and I don't want to look in the mirror."

Then I look in the mirror and describe what I see: "That face does not look happy. That is an angry-looking face. I do not like feeling angry; I don't want to know what I might be angry about. I really blew it yesterday with the boss. Today I can't even figure out what to wear. I'd like to cancel my dental appointment." I continue in that vein until I become bored or run out of time, and I conclude with the statement: "I unconditionally accept myself with all my weaknesses and shortcomings."

Like many other human beings, I don't have much difficulty acknowledging the facts of the situations I find myself in, but often neglect to look at the feelings I may have about those facts. Whenever I sucker myself by feeling smug because I'm not denying the facts, I often get clobbered by the hidden feelings that sneak up on me. Just because I understand and accept things doesn't mean that I don't have to feel them. But unacknowledged feelings often lead to a relapse.

Coping with Relapse

Profound self-acceptance includes the acceptance of relapse and avoids moral judgments—good or bad. This kind of self-acceptance does not condone negative or destructive behavior; it simply says "Yes, this is what I am doing" or have done.

For example, although I lost more than eighty pounds while I was involved with OA and kept it off for many years, it began to creep back after a serious romance failed. I had faced up to the fact that the relationship had been impossible and had painfully extricated myself, but I didn't fully admit how deeply I'd been hurt.

Ten years later I'd regained all the lost weight plus an extra twenty pounds. During that time I'd begun to practice profound self-acceptance toward myself, including my body and my eating habits. I had finally realized that the fat itself wasn't as bad as condemning myself for being fat; my blood pressure, cholesterol count, and general health remained excellent. Also, I no longer was eating unconsciously, but choosing what I ate and at times experiencing choosing to overeat.

I finally accepted that I may be fat forever. If so, I was willing to be fat and happy. That does not mean I was happy about being fat, just willing to be happy no matter what. Then I started making a few changes in my eating habits—not dieting, not trying to lose weight, but just making different choices. And slowly, so slowly I hardly noticed it, I began to lose the weight the same way I'd regained it—a pound or so a week. That weight loss coincided with the intense creative involvement of the early stages of writing this book. Within a year I lost fifty pounds. During that year it was a constant astonishment to me that I was losing at all, because I ate whatever I wanted and experienced no sense of deprivation.

With an attitude of profound self-acceptance toward relapse, it's possible to admit a slip or recognize a symptom of the old behavior or thinking pattern immediately. It's possible to view that behavior as unuseful and counterproductive, and sometimes to halt it before total disaster or an out-of-control binge ensues. It's also possible to accept the devastation of a binge and not have to compound it with self-hate.

If the slip has a physically addictive component, such as alcohol, sugar, salt, or nicotine, people who know themselves also know what will follow. With self-knowledge and self-acceptance, they can tolerate the addictive response, the craving for more, or the allergic reactions and not have to give in, but just wait for the reaction to pass.

Relapse, or a slip, may be inevitable if you're dealing with the kind of recovery where total abstinence is not possible. Total abstinence from food or from human relationships, for example, may work in the short term, but not in the long haul. Fasting or isolation can aid self-awareness temporarily, but does not provide a useful long-term model for joyful living.

Programs for those with eating disorders or those who are in abusive relationships require a lot of emphasis on profound self-acceptance so that the participants won't use the program as another form of self-abuse. The low self-esteem of the over-eater or people-pleaser is often reflected in a downcast "I'm sure you know best" or a defiant "I'm the worst" attitude.

On the other hand, the grandiosity of the alcoholic is ex-emplified by a cocky "I'm the best" facade. These differences make the AA model for recovery, which is increasingly popular for all kinds of problems, work best for addictions like alcoholism, where total abstinence is possible. Unfortunately, the concept of total abstinence often takes people from the complacency of denial to the pain of perfectionism. When one slip is promoted as a return to the depths of a progressive disease, the mental and emotional emphasis on doing it right can lead to trouble and contribute to relapse. Profound self-acceptance counteracts perfectionism through its emphasis on not being judgmental.

Profound self-acceptance includes the cultivation of com-passion for oneself as a fallible and struggling human being, especially when relapse occurs. We always do the best we can. Sometimes I don't like knowing that, but the vain regret of "I could have done better" is a trap that denies the truth. Admit-ting the truth of "This is what I did, and I don't feel good about it" can lead the way to other truths that can help me to avoid future relapse.

Difficulty in accepting ourselves as imperfect human beings or resisting the idea of profound self-acceptance often comes from old belief systems. Core beliefs come from personal, family, and cultural influences. These beliefs must be chal-lenged before we can become who we are.

Challenging Your Beliefs

Our beliefs affect and govern the way we live and are an important way for us to know about the world. Beliefs come from a variety of sources. Some are myths we accept without direct here-and-now experience, because we trust the source of that information. Those kinds of beliefs can deter us from direct experience and keep us stuck. Other beliefs are founded on our direct experience.

Beliefs feed thoughts and feelings. According to Janet Burr, author of *Awaken Your Intuition*, "A thought held too long becomes an opinion, then a belief." For instance, Jane believed that she was unlovable and rejected people who loved her with the thought, "I wonder what's wrong with them?" Having that belief colored her view of the world and her experiences.

At the beginning of her recovery from alcoholism, Debbie, the cocktail waitress, had tended to see the world through rose-colored glasses. Jane tended to believe that "Nothing good ever happens to me." Her immediate reaction to any positive event was, "You must be kidding," as if she viewed the situation through doubt-colored glasses.

Beliefs are often unconscious, but giving up part of a belief that doesn't work today can enable us to experience life as fresh and new. Being driven by unconscious beliefs, or holding on to old beliefs, often sets us up for continued relapse, disappointment, or frustration. Limiting beliefs function like straitjackets that restrict movement and curtail possibilities.

The following self-scoring quiz can help you discover some beliefs that may be adversely affecting your life.

Creative Process #4
True/False Beliefs

Mark these statements true or false.

_____ I hate making mistakes.
_____ Security is very important to me.

_____ I usually don't enjoy my job.

_____ I don't trust other people very much.

_____ I'm often afraid people won't like me.

_____ I have trouble making friends.

_____ I'll do anything to keep things harmonious.

_____ I often feel guilty and remorseful.

_____ I can't stand looking foolish.

_____ I'm not a pessimist; I'm a realist.

_____ I often feel inadequate.

_____ I think people are untrustworthy.

_____ I'd rather be right than be happy.

_____ I usually put other's needs ahead of my own.

_____ I can't stand to have to wait for anything.

_____ I'm seldom really happy.

_____ People don't often appreciate the things I do for them.

_____ My parents could have done better than they did.

_____ I'm often misunderstood.

_____ I think happy people just don't understand what's going on.

_____ I seldom can just relax and have fun.

_____ I'm often afraid people will find out what I'm really like.

_____ I'm always polite, no matter how I feel.

_____ I find it really difficult to trust the opposite sex.

Scoring: Every statement you marked as true may reflect a belief that can create problems for you. If you marked eight to fourteen as true, negative beliefs may be eroding your quality of life. If you agree with fourteen or more of the statements, your commitment to avoiding the possibility of embarrassment, rejection, or disappointment may keep you safe, but may limit your participation in your own life.

No matter what your score, this is simply more information. It should be empowering rather than making you feel bad in any way especially if you can begin to cultivate an attitude of profound self-acceptance.

Food for Thought

Your answers aren't important here, just your feelings.

- If improving yourself hasn't really worked, are you willing to give up trying and accept yourself just the way you are?
- If not, what would it take for you to accept yourself unconditionally?
- What level of profound self-acceptance are you operating from today?
- Are you more tolerant of others than of yourself?
- Are you able to face the facts of your life?
- Are you willing to look for the feelings about the facts of your life, and face them?
- Are you willing to challenge some of your beliefs?

· 5 ·

Powerful People Don't
Defend, Explain,
or Justify

*Now it is a funny thing about life. If you refuse to accept
anything but the best you very often get it; if you utterly
decline to make do with what you can get, then somehow or other you are likely to get what you want.*

SOMERSET MAUGHAM

OWER MEANS the ability to do or act—to be able. Powerful people don't *dexify* (defend, explain, or justify).
They have done the work to find out what they really
want, and they refuse to accept anything less than the best. So
the real questions become, What do you want to be able to do
or be? and What do you want to be able to feel or enjoy?

Powerful people identify what's behind the false self-
improvement agenda initiated by the visible or immediate
problems—problems such as overspending or staying in an
abusive relationship. Although curbing spending or getting
out of harm's way can be part of a useful agenda, healthy
people go beyond superficial solutions to determine what the
underlying or real problems are—problems such as envy,

perfectionism, or lack of self-worth. This clears the way toward knowing what they want to do or be, to feel or enjoy. This knowledge creates satisfaction and leads to happiness.

Recovery that focuses only on controlling symptoms, such as the use of addictive substances or compulsive behavior, creates difficulty in living in harmony with oneself. In addition, it breeds dissatisfaction and a chronic sense of not-enoughness—of both not-getting-enough and not-being-enough. These attitudes invalidate personal power.

Advice on Advice

Everyone has personal power, and most of us habitually give it away by defending, explaining, or justifying ourselves. Many people give their power away to their therapists, support groups, or friends. One way they give it away is by chronically asking others for advice. If you ask someone for advice, and that person is unwise enough to offer it, one of two things usually happens. Either you don't like the advice, but try to follow it anyway, figuring that that person must know better than you do. Or you don't like the advice and argue about it, insisting on all the reasons it won't work for you. (By the way, every time you say more than two sentences in explanation of something, you have taken a defensive position—especially if you volunteer the information.)

Here's what happens next. If you've given away your power, you may try to follow the advice without determining its suitability for you. If it really doesn't feel right to you, however, one way or another you will unconsciously sabotage whatever effort you make. That unconscious sabotage makes it impossible to take any advice you really don't agree with. Then you can feel guilty, justifying your poor results with the excuse "I really didn't try hard enough." Or, you can use that experience of failure to further devalue yourself. And the person you asked for advice may collaborate in helping you do both, if he or she is insecure or needs to be right.

Every time you say more than two sentences
in explanation of something you have taken
a defensive position.

If you argue about the advice you're given, then the advisor gets to tell you all the reasons why it should work anyway. And if you don't give in, or give up and do it that way, the person can accuse you of being in resistance.

There's a difference between "That doesn't feel right for me," and "I don't feel like doing that right now." Pay attention to when your experience, or your intuition, tells you that something is not useful or healthy for you to do. Sometimes, however, it's important just to go through the motions. For instance, I know that taking a daily walk is a vital part of my well-being, but some days I don't feel like going out. Any excuse will do. If I know I'll feel better afterwards, then sometimes I can encourage myself do it anyway.

It's preferable, of course, not to give your power away. You are the real expert on you. No one else can truly know what is best for you. Blindly or unthinkingly following anyone else's advice, the dogma of any group, or the shoulds of society only creates pain and frustration, delaying your finding out who you really are.

One way to reclaim your power when someone interrupts you with unasked-for advice is to quietly stop the other person and say, "I don't want advice. I just want you to listen." And when you are interrupted again, patiently repeat, "I don't want you to fix it. I just want you to listen."

Sometimes advice produces a sigh of relief and an I-wish-I'd-thought-of-that-myself response. The most interesting fact about advice is that people seldom really want advice—even when they request it. Advice, even good advice, has a hook in it: If the advice is followed and is useful, the advice-giver gets part of the credit; if the advice is bad, the advice-giver gets blamed. That kind of communication can burden a relationship.

Sometimes people just need information. The difference between information and advice is the attachment the giver has to what the recipient does with it. Information is offered; advice is volunteered or pushed. Information is neutral; advice is loaded with feelings.

Denial of Power Creates Resentment

People like Aaron, who suffered burn-out working in the insurance field, distrust most advice because they don't trust themselves. In addition, they often deny that they have any power. Unacknowledged power is dangerous; like a child with a loaded gun who thinks it's a toy, anything can happen. Denial of personal power is as irresponsible as thinking of oneself as omnipotent.

Denial of personal power results in defensiveness, over-explaining, and compulsive justification of all feelings and acts. Aaron's defensiveness, however, manifested itself in long silences, and most of his justification occurred only in his thoughts. His silences came across as a holier-than-thou attitude of righteousness, which often alienated even his best friends.

On the other hand, Jane tended to overexplain and to be too agreeable. One symptom of approval-addiction is over-explaining, a common problem for many women. Jane, who needed constant confirmation that she was okay, had learned to be agreeable and a people-pleaser who automatically deferred to others rather than express her preferences.

People like Jane and Aaron, who give their power away, often have trouble with time. Jane, always ten to fifteen minutes late, was always apologetic, full of explanations. Aaron was always a half-hour early and worried that he'd be late. Irresponsibility versus rigidity. One sign of immaturity is the inability to gauge the time it will take to do a task. "Everything always takes twice as long as my most realistic estimate," Fred would say every time he was late, flashing his most charming smile.

Playing doormat, scapegoat, victim, or otherwise giving your power away results in the silent and tyrannical martyrdom of "Look what I did for you. Now you owe me." Both Aaron and Jane, suffering from a lack of trust in themselves, lived lives of deference, self-pity, and resentment rather than lives of autonomy and responsibility.

Beyond superficial self-improvement lies a median ground where one is usually on time, occasionally late, and sometimes early, but where there is no guilt, no anxiety, no explaining, no excuses. This median ground of flexibility is a position of power.

The Nine Positions of Power

One of the nine power positions is the ability to remain flexible—not to get stuck in either a perfectionistic or apologetic stance. People with flexibility can tolerate making mistakes, because they are usually willing to view mistakes as learning experiences.

Three other positions of power are nonresistance, neutrality, and detachment. Nonresistance eliminates the need to defend, explain, or justify; the nonresistant person isn't interested in being right or in making others wrong. Maintaining an attitude of neutrality reduces expectations and negative comparisons or judgments. The neutral person is willing to have things work out without dictating how that will happen. Detachment enables a person to let go of results—to be able to separate from emotional considerations or the personalities involved. When these kinds of control issues are minimized, a person cannot be manipulated and is not interested in manipulating others.

Power also comes from humility, tolerance, and honesty. Humility is the ability to admit you don't know everything and includes the willingness to risk making a fool of yourself. Tolerance doesn't mean always agreeing with everyone; it means accepting other people and divergent opinions without invalidating one's own point of view. Honesty provides the foundation for developing many of these qualities, because telling yourself and others the truth always leads to self-knowledge.

Self-knowledge is the penultimate power position, because the more you are willing to know about yourself, the more you know about other people.

The last position of power is persistence. When you have the willingness to do whatever it takes, when you're not easily discouraged, when you don't know how to give up, you can accomplish just about anything. Those who make it in any endeavor are those who often don't have sense enough to quit.

> *The more you are willing to know about yourself*
> *the more you know about other people.*

The Value of Talking Things Out

Geraldine, a compulsive gambler, had a unique method for getting brief therapy without defending, explaining, or justifying herself. Although she kept a journal on a regular basis, sometimes she needed to talk things out. She kept a ten-dollar bill in her purse for just such a purpose. She always picked a grocery store away from her neighborhood, collected twelve to fifteen small items, and when the clerk at the checkout stand asked "How are you today?", she passionately recited her current problems in full, gory detail. Usually the clerk gave her a startled-doe look and proceeded to ring up her purchases in record time.

Geraldine saved her family and friends from getting dumped on, saved herself fifty dollars in therapy fees, and figured she had given the clerk a great weird-customer story to share with co-workers. Needless to say, she never returned to the same store twice.

Taxi drivers, hairdressers, and bartenders have long served for this kind of unofficial therapy—that of talking things out and of being "witnessed." The act of confession in the Catholic church also functions in this way. Once, when I was out of town, several of my students left long messages on my answering machine. They reported feeling much better about whatever they had wanted my help with, even though they knew I wouldn't hear their messages until much later.

Judith, during an unhappy time in her marriage, volunteered for a weekend shift on the phones at her local crisis hotline. Her volunteer service paid an unexpected bonus when, after weeks of listening to people in crisis, she realized that there seemed to be two kinds of callers: people who had real problems like cancer or no place to live, and others who just seemed to make trouble for themselves. Judith's insight enabled her to sort out her own difficulties, to figure out when she was just making trouble for herself and when she had real problems and needed to express her feelings in her therapy group.

Author Anais Nin, who kept an extensive diary, wrote,

> Expressing feeling is directly linked with creation. My telling all to the diary helped me in this. . . . Try to write in your diary to keep that little flame burning. Expand, open, speak, name, describe, exclaim, paint, caricature, dance, jump in your writing. We are here . . . to say everything. Speak for your moods, make your muteness and silence eloquent.

Which is best: dumping things out as Geraldine does, listening to others' troubles as Judith does, writing things down as Anais Nin did, or getting feedback from a friend, teacher, or therapist? All of them work. They help us listen to ourselves, to get our difficulties and confused feelings out of the confines of our minds and bodies, to help us gain some distance or perspective. Aaron cheated himself of perspective and feedback by his silences.

Feedback is something we are used to getting from other people or from our environment; a friend tells us how hurtful our humor is; the electric company threatens to turn off the lights if we don't pay our bills. However, we don't usually think of feedback or good information as something we can reliably provide for ourselves. Most people with problems have lost some trust in themselves and their ability to figure things out. Many Creative Processes in this book are designed to renew that trust as well as provide specific ways to obtain information from the past and to access intuition or inner wisdom.

How do you know when it's really your intuition? Whenever a relationship turned sour, Elaina complained, "So often I've thought it was good intuition, but it turned out just to be bad judgment." Others in support groups have found themselves caught up in living out someone else's idea of how they should behave, which can interfere with healthy living. Reliable do-it-yourself feedback, however, is possible using the next Creative Process.

Understanding Your Feelings

Feelings need to be felt and expressed. The goal for those in recovery is to feel what we feel and to know what we know. Unfortunately, feelings don't seem to be all that simple to figure out. Part of the difficulty is that not only do we have feelings, but we have feelings about our feelings! For instance, Elaina gets a call from her best friend who just won a trip to Hawaii. Elaina, feeling happy for her friend, says, "Hey, that's great!" But when she hangs up she feels envious, then feels guilty for feeling envious. Which is the true feeling?

Well, it's likely that all three feelings are genuine at the moment she experienced them, and it's important to acknowledge and accept them all. Uncovering all the levels of feelings is part of the task and the key to reclaiming our power.

How do we uncover all our true feelings? How can we express them without creating havoc and devastation for ourselves? If expressing feelings means that Elaina tells her friend that she's feeling envious and guilty, what will that do to their relationship? Are Elaina's feelings her friend's responsibility?

Are relationships the right place to dump feelings? How can we learn to trust ourselves again?

One way is by using your journal, your notebook, or your tape recorder to express the jumble of feelings and to sort them out before deciding which ones are appropriate to share with others.

The following simple technique is designed to bring feelings into the open and consists of picking an object or a thing, then writing or speaking from its point of view in a stream-of-consciousness outpouring. This Creative Process is the most versatile, most exciting, and most powerful one I've ever used. It's limited only by the scope of your imagination. If you were to keep a daily record for a year using only this technique, you would find it both worthwhile and fascinating.

Creative Process #5
Stream-of-Consciousness

This process may seem silly if you just read it and neglect to try it out. I urge you to invest a few minutes in experiencing this powerful tool for awareness. Use your notebook or tape recorder; play with it mentally for a few minutes before going on.

1. Pick any object in the room, or in view, or in your mind's eye. You could pick the lamp, the rug, a favorite possession, the teddy bear you had as a child, the watch on your wrist. You could even choose an item that represents power to you, such as your automobile, your checkbook, or your fancy leather briefcase.

2. Pretend you are the chosen object and, using your tape recorder or notebook, let the object talk about itself. When you begin to record or write, keep going without stopping to figure anything out. Aim for a stream-of-consciousness flow of words—not censoring or holding back. If you get stuck or just feel foolish, use the flow of words to talk about that feeling before you get back on track.

Start by letting the object name or describe itself: "I am Jean's wristwatch and I keep track of time for her." Think of yourself as taking dictation from that object. Have some fun with it. Don't think about how to do it; just allow yourself to ramble on for two to twelve minutes. If you get totally stuck, just keep repeating "I feel stuck, I feel stuck, I feel stuck" until the time is up or you get back on track.

3. After the object has told you as much as possible about itself, talk to it. Ask it questions. Record its answers. Use it as a confidante, a Dear Abby; see what advice or feedback it has for you.

4. When you're finished, play back or read what you've done. The purpose is to hear what you had to say—to see how you are thinking and feeling at this moment in time, and to claim those thoughts and feelings as your own. The feedback and answers you get in this way tend to be more reliable than those which come from outside sources, no matter how well-meaning.

How This Creative Process Works

This process works because it allows us to express our innermost thoughts and feelings without taking full responsibility for them. "It's not me saying that, it's my wristwatch." We project our thoughts and feelings onto the inanimate object. This kind of projection is not something we need to learn; it's something we do all the time. Every time I think I know how you feel, I'm projecting. Every time I think I know what you're thinking about me, I'm projecting. Using projection deliberately, as a technique, will be new for some of us and is one way of experiencing our personal power.

Using an inanimate object coupled with a stream-of-consciousness outpouring seems to tap into the subconscious, to skim off that top layer of thoughts and feelings that is just below the level of conscious awareness. What I like best about this versatile process is that even though I've figured out how it works, it works for me every time I surrender just to doing it and getting involved in a playful way. It serves as a barometer for how I really feel at that moment.

For example, if today I choose the rug in my office for a stream-of-consciousness projection, it may begin something like this: "I am the beautiful old oriental-type rug in Jean's Seattle office. Jean inherited me from Grandma Bryant and she loves the faded magenta and blue and beige colors in my design. I am often surrounded by the many interesting groups of people that Jean leads. I love being the center of attention and enjoy the compliments that people often give me."

Tomorrow I could pick the same focus for doing a projection, and the rug may say, "I am the faded old threadbare rug that Jean has on her office floor, and I've had a lot of things spilled on me over the years. What bothers me the most, though, is that all people do is walk on me."

You can see the difference in emotional tone between the two examples; the first reflects high self-esteem, the second sounds full of self-pity.

This technique results in gaining indirect-sourced material. Information gained this lighthearted way comes from the creative right brain, which appreciates fun and humor. The right brain is the seat of emotions, and this kind of information is often more reliable as an emotional barometer than direct questions, which tend to be answered by the intellect.

For example, if someone asks "Why did you do that?", it not only creates defensiveness but also takes the prize for the least useful direct question asked of oneself or of anyone. The intellect, or left brain, defends, explains, justifies; it answers that kind of question with explanations, reasons, or rationalizations that usually have little to do with authentic feelings. The intellect is useful for practical, logistical problem solving, such as how to get from one side of the city to the other or how to fill out a tax form. The intellect makes lists of pros and cons and tries to figure things out. In contrast, feelings are meant to be experienced and expressed rather than figured out.

Experiencing Your Feelings

Figuring out how feelings work in your life, however, can increase your personal power. The hierarchy of feelings begins with feelings of fear or hurt. When you fear losing somebody or something, anxiety stirs; when you experience the loss, your hurt feelings surface. When you deny or discount that hurt, the feelings manifest as anger; when you deny or ignore anger, you feel guilty; when guilt is unacknowledged, you feel depressed. Therefore, when I begin to feel guilty or depressed, I've learned to ask myself the key questions: What am I afraid of? What happened that made me feel hurt?

Because feelings follow this predictable pattern, if I take care of my fear, hurt, and anger, I won't have to feel guilty or depressed. Guilt and depression are ways of avoiding the responsibility of experiencing our feelings of loss and hurt and avoiding the ownership of our personal power.

Guilt can also be a form of image management: To behave badly is a sin. To behave badly and not feel guilty about it, especially in today's society, is to compound that sin. But if I sin and feel guilty, it shows that I know better. Therefore, I'm pretending that I'm a better person than I really am—judging by my behavior.

For example, I'm on a diet and eating dinner out with friends; when dessert is offered and I can't resist, I could simply admit "I really can't resist that" or "I love chocolate chip cookies" and enjoy the sweet. Instead, I protest falsely: "I know I shouldn't be doing this" or "This is delicious, but I feel so guilty." These statements are attempts at image management of manipulating your opinion of my behavior. I'm hoping you will think better of me, if I admit feeling guilty.

After all, in today's world, what's worse than being overweight and publicly indulging your sweet tooth? The fat person who eats forbidden sweets without caring what society thinks ends up being heavily censured especially if that person obviously doesn't feel guilty about it. In general, we tend to be more understanding and forgiving of those who claim to feel remorse in this kind of situation.

Nevertheless, the most detrimental aspect of this false remorse is perpetuating hypocrisy and denial of responsibility for our true intentions and actions. That denial can mask real problems. One trait Judith disliked in her mother was what seemed to be a contradiction between the values she paid lip service to and how she behaved. For example, her mother condemned gossiping, but often was the first to spread a rumor by mentioning it on the phone to her best friend, whom she knew could never keep anything to herself. Judith's mother felt guilty when that happened, but didn't stop gossiping. The guilt enabled her not only to continue denying how this habit fed her need for attention, but also to neglect her power to create a more interesting life for herself.

Guilt Versus Happiness

The Creative Processes in this book coupled with an ongoing commitment to self-examination help us to identify our real problems. Katherine Mansfield, at the end of her journal, wrote, "I want by understanding myself, to understand others. I want to be all I'm capable of becoming. . . . This all sounds very strenuous and serious. But now that I have wrestled with it, it's no longer so. I feel happy—deep down. All is well."

It's true that the more you understand and accept in yourself, the more you understand and accept in others. This understanding and acceptance can transform relationships quicker than the time-honored method of guilt-induced self-sacrifice. Allowing yourself to feel happy without feeling guilty is a position of power, especially if the people you live with or care about are troubled. Elaina, a former Valium abuser, had a basically happy nature; she loved gardening and after her recovery spent a lot of time with her hands in the dirt among the roses she loved and nurtured and knew by name. She often sang to herself as she worked.

She felt guilty about her happiness because her newly re-tired husband was depressed and her daughter was using co-caine. She felt powerless to control them or to make them happy. Therefore, she thought that all she could do for them was to suppress her own happiness, even though that sacrifice changed nothing for them. I suggested that she write herself a permission slip—telling herself it was okay to be happy even if her family wasn't. I encouraged her not to flaunt her happi-ness, or to conceal it, or to feel guilty about it.

This change of attitude created a great deal of discomfort for her at first; she tended to feel guilty for not feeling guilty. However, her willingness to enjoy her small pleasures without guilt set a good example for the others in the family and mea-surably increased her quality of life. Although her husband continued to be depressive, eventually her daughter began therapy, and one day she said to Elaina, "Mom, when I saw that you were able to be happy even though you were worried about me and Dad, I felt there might be hope for me."

Food for Thought

Some items to consider, to play with, to speculate about:

- What's your guilt quotient?
- Do other people's moods control your moods?
- Do you volunteer information or overexplain?
- Do you often defend or justify what you're doing?
- Do you let other people define who you are or interpret and analyze your motives?
- Are you comfortable admitting you don't know all the answers?
- Do you allow yourself to feel what you feel and to know what you know?
- Do you set limits with yourself and with others?
- Are you willing to be happy?

·6·

Making Friends with
Your Rebel and
Your Seeker

There is a vitality, a life force, an energy, a quickening, that is translated through you into action. And, because there is only one of you in all time, this expression is unique. . . . It is not your business to determine how good it is, nor how valuable, nor how it compares with other expressions. It is your business to keep it yours clearly, and directly. MARTHA GRAHAM

VITALITY and unique expression emerge from self-knowledge and profound self-acceptance. Vitality and unique expression lead to free-flowing and purposeful action. When we stop judging and comparing our many selves and make it our business to make friends with them instead, our energy remains clear and direct.

We all have within us many selves, selves that emerge in the process of self-discovery. Each self has its own voice and its own agenda. According to psychologists Hal Stone and Sidra Winkelman, "The selves we do not honor grow inside of us in unconscious ways, gaining power and authority." Each reflects our hereditary traits as well as beliefs, habits, and attitudes we've been taught by our family and the society we grew up in. Our rebellious selves, our seeking selves, and many other aspects and traits combine to make up our total personality. Unfortunately, those aspects and traits are often first interpreted and named by the people to whom we give our power.

The Power of Naming

Naming is a powerful act. Calling you "stupid," or "alcoholic," or "compulsive," or "macho" can be a way for someone to gain control over you. And when you call yourself those names, you reinforce that named self. Naming is also the way we attempt to control our world and our reality by interpreting what we see and by trying to understand who we are. In one of my journal-writing groups, Geraldine complained of "a lot of chaos I haven't bothered to name." Chaos was the name she'd already given it.

In addition, when temporary coping mechanisms become deeply integrated, they can take on a life of their own even after they seem to have outlived their usefulness. When these habits and addictions are named, they become part of our identity. Judith named her procrastinator self; Katy became a chocoholic. The struggle begins when we reject, deny, try to get rid of, or otherwise resist any part of ourselves, named or unnamed; we can remain stuck in perpetual conflict with ourselves.

Coping with Resistance

What you resist, persists. Therefore, one way to initiate change is to drop the resistance by surrendering to the reality of the moment. Surrendering is one of the things that happens when you engage in profound self-acceptance. The principle of nonresistance always produces change. Nonresistance is much easier said than done, however, because it's human nature to resist anything that threatens the status quo.

Last week, for instance, I headed out for my daily walk,

hoping to return before the predicted rainstorm. As I approached the farthest point of my three-mile circuit, it began to mist, then to drizzle. Then it began to rain in earnest, and I saw no shelter until it was over. I spent the next few uncomfortable minutes trying to protect my head and the back of my neck from the chilling downpour. I resisted in vain as my leather shoes and my jeans and my sweatshirt became soaked and heavy. When there was no way I could get any wetter, I relaxed, surrendered to my soggy reality, began to stride more briskly, and found myself enjoying the day—rain and all.

I'd like to think I will remember that episode the next time I'm resisting the inevitable or fighting with myself. Hannah, in an evening journal group, observed, "One thing I've learned from experience is that I don't always learn from experience." That's also true for me.

Even though I now understand the principle of nonresistance, it's proved to be impossible just to stop resisting. Resistance cannot be willed away, especially if I'm trying to will it away to manipulate myself into changing. Paradoxically, it's important not to resist even my resistance and to befriend both the resistance and that which I'm resisting.

I'm helped in doing this through the power of acknowledgment; when in doubt, I acknowledge the obvious. "Yes, I'm feeling lazy today. And I'm trying to make myself get to work. And I don't like feeling lazy. But resisting being lazy isn't helping." I usually end each statement I make by saying the word "acknowledgment" as a reminder to accept my thoughts and feelings rather than to judge them.

Sometimes I take a defiant attitude toward what I'm acknowledging. "Okay, so I'm feeling lazy today. So what? And I wish I could change myself from being a lazy slug to being Superwoman. So what?" Another tactic is to wallow in it, to really get into the spirit of being lazy, to be thoroughly lazy, to be lazy with style and grace, to turn being lazy into an art form. Then, when I become bored with that, I switch to wallowing in my resistance, to think of it as a new Olympic sport for which I set the standards.

Creative Process #6
What's the Problem?

Here's a different method to help you stop resisting your own reality, to make friends with all the parts, named and unnamed, that you encounter within yourself, to mediate those inner conflicts, and to begin an organic process to initiate integration. It's a seven-part process, and you don't have to do it all at once unless you want to. However, you will probably obtain more powerful results if you are willing to set aside the better part of an hour and just do it. Each section can take five to ten minutes, but it's better if you get involved with the spirit of the process and lose track of time.

1. Using your notebook or tape recorder, take five to ten minutes to quickly list some things you like about yourself and some of the habits, characteristics, and tendencies that you don't like about yourself—the things you consider to be a problem, difficulty, or handicap. We all experience problems and difficulties; we all have handicaps, not just obvious physical disabilities, but things about ourselves that we don't want others to find out about. A handicap is anything you experience as a handicap, anything you think is a handicap, or anything that the world agrees is a handicap.

   Include at least three things you like about yourself for each one you don't like. The items on the lists needn't be big things: "I like my curly hair." "I'm kind to animals." "One problem is I never write to my mother." "My thighs are humongous."

   Some things on your lists may be traits about yourself that you don't like, but do accept as part of who you are. Other items will be behaviors you don't really accept and have often tried to control—your so-called bad habits. Include some areas that you have repeatedly tried to improve or change: "I can't quit smoking." "I'm always late." "I let people walk all over me." "I wish I could lose fifteen pounds." "I drink too much coffee."

   See if you can find twelve to fifteen items ranging from

the serious, such as perfectionism, alcoholism, or compulsive gambling, to the not-so-serious.

2. When you reach a stopping place with your lists, pick one difficulty, problem, or habit you've repeatedly tried to fix, improve, or get rid of—something you'd be willing to change your experience of.

3. For another five to ten minutes, use the stream-of-consciousness process from the previous chapter to allow the part of yourself that performs the so-called bad habit—the rebel self—to express itself in its own words. Think of yourself as taking dictation from that part of yourself. Allow it to tell you about itself, to introduce itself to you. Mine thinks of itself as a rebel because it's always acting out and getting into trouble. Allow yours to tell you some positive things about itself and to say what it likes about itself. Chances are it won't describe itself as bad.

4. Again for five to ten minutes allow the other part—the one that pushes for improvement and change, the seeker self—to express itself in its own words. Allow it to tell you its name or what it prefers to be called. Finish by allowing that part to say what it's most afraid of. Chances are it has its own unique fears and desires.

5. Take five to ten minutes to record a discussion between them about their areas of disagreement. Each will no doubt see the problem differently.

6. The following series of questions is addressed to the seeker self—the part that seeks the change. The word "you" or "yourself" refers to the seeker self, not to you the whole person. Write or speak the question, then allow the seeker to answer immediately and automatically. Don't predict or control the responses; just record them. Aim for that stream-of-consciousness flow, first with the question, then the response.

- What specifically do you want for yourself?
- How does that other part—the rebel—stop you from getting what you want for yourself?
- Is there any way the rebel part could be of any use to you?

- What would happen if the rebel part went away completely? How would this help you?
- Do you know what the rebel part wants?
- What would happen if you allowed the rebel part to have what it wants?
- Is it possible there's a way you both could get what you want?
- Would you be willing to continue to explore that possibility with the rebel part?

7. If the answer is yes, resume the discussion between the two parts. Think of yourself as taking dictation as they negotiate.

The more familiar we become with all aspects of ourselves, the more we will understand that each part of us experiences itself as doing something *for* us. Even the rebellious parts that act out in destructive ways usually think of themselves as protecting us from something worse. If we can accept this, then we have a better chance of living in harmony with our many selves, and we can spontaneously give up or modify behavior that no longer is necessary for survival.

When Sarah did this process, for example, her hungry rebel who overeats referred to its behavior as comforting and protecting her from feeling hurt; she'd never thought of it as anything but bad until that time. After recognizing its helpful intent, Sarah stopped feeling guilty when she ate too much. Eventually, she found herself not overeating as often.

Renaming the Symptom

Judith discovered another way to initiate organic change. For many years her perfectionism and tendency to self-analysis had collaborated to produce elaborate self-improvement projects. She identified, or thought she identified, many self-destructive habits or fatal flaws in her character. Because these character defects were unacceptable to her, conflict was inevitable. She felt perpetually at war with herself. "My head is out to get me," she'd quip, when she'd catch herself rationalizing her current obsession, or, "Procrastination sabotages my efforts."

The battles with herself absorbed a lot of energy, and she never experienced a moment's rest from the conflict. There seemed to be so many areas where one part of her indulged in a certain kind of behavior, such as watching too many soap operas or putting off things that needed to be done, and the other part devised elaborate, and futile, plans to stop that behavior.

For more than ten years *Stop Procrastinating* was first on Judith's self-improvement list. One year she decided to take it off her list because other, more important areas needed improving. She also had seen little progress in overcoming that problem and noticed that despite procrastinating she did accomplish quite a few things she wanted to do not as much as she could have, of course, but, as a freelance graphic artist, she had learned to live with the crisis of deadlines.

She would delay working on an assignment as long as possible while feeling constantly guilty. At the critical mass point—24 to 36 hours before a project was due—she'd panic and suddenly become very motivated. She'd grab her favorite pencil and set to work furiously, crashing the job out as fast as possible, but always completing it at the last possible moment. Each time she feared she wouldn't finish it at all or that the work would be unacceptable.

Often those fears proved groundless, so she not only dropped the resolution off her list, but she also started bragging to her friends about being a world-class procrastinator. She'd laugh and claim that it was a very exciting way to live, that she wasn't really a procrastinator as much as a very efficient deadline worker.

Perfectionists like Judith often procrastinate because the pressure of a deadline forces them to abandon or give up the necessity of doing it right in favor of getting it done. Only when there was not time enough to do it perfectly could Judith allow herself to do it at all. This behavior is often coupled with the illusion that, as Judith often explained, "I could have done it better if I'd had more time."

Within six months after dropping *Stop Procrastinating* from her list, something very peculiar happened. With some astonishment she became aware that she was completing more assignments in a timely manner and that no longer could she claim world-class status as a procrastinator. When she stopped pushing herself to change, when she stopped resisting her own disorganized and innovative ways of getting things done, when she fully accepted her tendency to procrastinate, her behavior moderated.

In essence she'd dropped resistance to her unorthodox and creative working habits and accepted things the way they were. What she hadn't realized was that her delaying tactics gave her creative subconscious a chance to work on the projects. Her casual, yet profound self-acceptance created a relaxed atmosphere, which led to natural change. Laughing and calling herself a world-class procrastinator removed expectations that it should be different. Change often takes place more easily on the edge of lightness.

In addition, she had done what psychologist John Enright calls "renaming the symptom." At the point that she referred to herself as a very efficient deadline worker rather than a procrastinator, she had renamed the symptom.

Renaming the symptom requires looking at the problem from a different, and usually more positive, point of view. If you can begin to appreciate that a habit you think of as bad also serves another purpose in your life, you have a better chance of living in harmony with your many selves.

Creative Process #7
What's in a Name?

This process can help you to transform or rename some of your rejected traits, not by getting rid of them or improving yourself, but by changing your perspective.

1. First, choose a negative symptom, habit, or trait, like laziness, stubbornness, procrastination, or selfishness. Pick one that's a little stale, one that's been around for a while.
2. Describe the actual behavior in a factual and relatively nonjudgmental way. Pretend you're playing charades. How would you act out the trait or behavior? Include both actions and thoughts. For instance, laziness could be described as "I sit and watch television even when the house needs cleaning" or "I can't get excited about cleaning house" or "I get so relaxed I forget what I'm supposed to be doing."
3. Now, think of a way to refer to what happens in a more positive way, a way that reflects some true value for you. Stubbornness and persistence, for example, can refer to the same behavior. Laziness could be viewed as a commitment to being relaxed. Experience is individual, and rarely do two people with the same symptom come up with the same new name. Sarah found that her *fat* renamed became a "warm cloak of visibility which protects me from sexual harassment." Selfishness could be called "a commitment to my own well-being despite other considerations." You'll know when you've found the right new name, because there's a tendency to grin with delight or smile with recognition at the moment of successful renaming.

Often traits that have negative connotations, or names, are those originally identified and named by someone else. It's important to understand that after you pass childhood, you are the one who gives both meaning and value to any event. The act of naming or renaming is also a way of reclaiming your personal power.

Nevertheless, I'm always astonished by how difficult this process of renaming can be and how hard I tend to cling to the original, and usually negative, interpretation. That's why this works best with traits that you're not too serious about or ones that you're overidentified with. When you experience the value of a different perspective and become more skilled in using this process, then you may be able to use it to gain insight into heavier character defects, addictions, or cross-addictions.

Renaming an addiction or character defect can help you lighten some of the grimness that often surrounds recovery issues.

Accepting Happiness

Grimness and unhappiness grow out of attitudes of rigidity, inflexibility, and distrust—seeing only one way to do things and seeing anybody who thinks differently as a potential enemy. Those who feel threatened by differences also discount their own, individual value. Never trying anything new, sticking to weary routines, and always doing what you think is expected of you contribute to boredom and isolation. Grimness and unhappiness also come from wishing you were something or somebody else.

On the other hand, happiness results from relating to people with realism and flexibility. Happiness includes the ability to accept what you are and know that it isn't so bad, and to express what you're feeling. Most importantly, happiness embraces humor, variety, and curiosity. The ability to become absorbed in intellectually challenging projects is a reflection of happiness.

Happiness does not ignore problems and handicaps, but enjoys provocative points of view about them: A problem is a goal that has manifested in your life, except you don't remember asking for it. A handicap is simply an asset you haven't figured out how to use yet. Judith's perfectionism handicapped her until she began to appreciate the deadline efficiency it created.

Once I remarked to Aaron that for me, there was no such thing as a bad experience—only good experiences and learning experiences.

He looked at me, then said, "Jean, there are such things as bad experiences."

"I know," I replied, "but you're a damn fool if you don't learn from them."

Although you cannot really learn any lesson from someone else's experiences, it's always possible to learn something from your own experiences.

After you pass childhood,
you are the one who gives both meaning
and value to any event.

What Is Selfishness?

My cousin Bruce, a hardworking law clerk, was recently chewed out by a supervisor for being chronically late to meetings. "You are a rude and selfish person to always make us wait for you," he was told.

"Am I a rude and selfish person," he asked me, "or is she just trying to show me who's boss? She could start without me if she wanted to." He felt locked into a power struggle with her.

"Selfishness," according to British novelist Ruth Rendell, "is not living as one wishes to live; it is asking others to live as one wishes to live." By that definition Bruce's supervisor was the selfish one. I reminded him that when people accuse you of being selfish, it simply means that you are not doing what they want you to do.

It's empowering to understand that they are also telling you something about themselves—their preferences, their values. In addition, they may also be telling you something about yourself, but not necessarily. However, if many people are giving you the same message, it may be useful to check it out, then decide what to do about it, if anything.

Bruce decided not to give his power away; however, he did admit that she had a point—he often was late. He also faced the reality that being chronically tardy is a real problem in the workplace. Bruce argued that in general he was kind and considerate, but he also acknowledged that his boss did have a right to be unhappy about his being late.

Despite her disapproval, Bruce still wasn't really concerned about his being ten minutes late. However, he refused to accept her definition of him as being rude and selfish. So, he made a point of being unfailingly pleasant to her whenever their paths crossed. Although he wasn't particularly successful in curing himself of being late, he did heal their relationship, and she eventually recommended him to head a project he really wanted.

If Bruce had continued to define the problem as a power struggle rather than as an honest difference in priorities, chances are they would still be fighting. The power position for Bruce was in not having to be right or in having to make his boss feel wrong. Naming or defining problems too quickly can create conflicts that often have nothing to do with the real issues.

Creative Process #8
Surrendering to Reality

The purpose of this process is to help you understand the dynamics underlying your so-called problems. It is one that Bruce could have used to shed some light on his problem.

1. First, describe a situation or a person that has the power to hurt you or to make you feel bad in some way. In the situation or the relationship with the person, see if you can find the exact stimulus that causes you the bad feeling. Make the description as specific as possible.

2. Now think of a person who is just like you, except that he or she doesn't react with hurt or pain to that stimulus. What would that person be like? Why wasn't the reaction the same as yours?

3. To what events or circumstances in your life can you trace your sensitivity? What happened to make you feel the way you feel in that situation?

4. How is it that you have continued to let yourself be hurt in this area? What does it do for you to remain sensitive to this stimulus? What would you have to give up, in what way would you be wrong, if you gave up sensitivity to this stimulus?

The point of this process is to gain information about yourself, not to coerce yourself to change or even to give up your negative reaction. If you obtain enough information and stumble upon the core truth about the situation, that alone will initiate some kind of change. However, this process is designed only to suggest some alternative points of view regarding the situation and will help you accept your current reality of it without having to change your relationship with it.

Every Problem Teaches a Lesson

Relationships with others and being friends with them takes time and energy. So does making friends with your many selves and learning the lessons they have to teach you. People who are willing to do these things ultimately find themselves both wiser and happier than others who live their lives on automatic—the ones who tend to believe that ignorance is bliss.

Wisdom for Jane included her bargain with Janie, the vulnerable five-year-old part of herself. One way she honored that bargain was to carry a rainbow-colored kite in the trunk of her car. Although Jane flew the kite only a few times a year, it served as a reminder of her commitment to Janie. Another way she cared for Janie was to play a cassette tape of lullabies when Janie needed soothing.

In addition, when Jane was on a stressful business trip to San Diego, she became aware that Janie needed attention. Janie wanted to go to the San Diego Zoo. Although Jane didn't much care for animals or zoos and felt too busy to go, she spent one morning being a friend to the Janie part of herself. She didn't want to relearn the lesson.

I resisted all possible lessons the November day I grabbed my sweater and letters to mail and rushed outside. As the door clicked behind me, I realized that I'd just locked myself out of my office. I felt stupid and angry. The day was cold, I had dozens of important things to do, and all my keys, including my car keys, were securely locked inside. I phoned my daughter, Deborah, from a nearby office, thinking she could pick me up and drive me home to get my spare keys; instead, I left a pitiful and incoherent message on her answering machine.

Cold and frustrated and not wanting to loiter around my office door, I headed for the coffee shop up the street. I was halfway there when I remembered that not only did I have no keys, but also I had no money with me. As I walked back to the office, I figured I may as well head for home; after all it was only a fifty-minute walk up the hill.

As I trudged along I stopped thinking "Why me?" and asked myself the more valuable question: "What am I experiencing that wouldn't be going on if this hadn't happened?" The answer was immediate. I grinned and settled into the walk I'd told myself I was too busy to fit into my schedule that day.

Being friends with yourself means knowing what questions to ask yourself when difficulties arise. Any of these questions can provide responses that may illuminate problems: How would my life be different if this hadn't happened? What am I experiencing that wouldn't be going on if this hadn't happened? If I was done with this lesson, what would I have learned? What is the name of this lesson?

Food for Thought

Seeking answers to the foregoing questions can produce awareness and can lead to insight and appreciation of that which you have created. Seeking answers to the questions below is not recommended. Nevertheless, paying attention to the feelings or emotions or images the questions evoke as you read them can be useful.

- Do your actions reflect your vitality?
- Is your life force, your energy, unblocked and free-flowing?
- Do you understand and appreciate your uniqueness?
- Can you resist the urge to sit in judgment on yourself?
- Have you given up comparing yourself, your selves, with others?
- Have you made friends with your many selves? Your rebel self? Your seeker self?
- Do you treat your many selves with as much compassion as you show your friends?
- Do you make it your business to keep your expressions, your actions, clear and direct?

·7·

Embracing the Shadows
of Your Past

One has to return again and again to weep the tears
which are still unshed. We cannot feel all the grief of
our many losses at the time we suffer them. That would
be too crippling. But if we would really gather our whole
lives into a single whole, no emotion that belongs to us
should be left unfelt.

IRENE CLAREMONT DE CASTILLEJO

T HE UNACKNOWLEDGED emotions that belong to us are
rooted in the past; self-esteem and recovery issues are
often connected to those unacknowledged emotions.
Many people seek to shut the door on the past or try in vain
to eliminate it, to get rid of its hidden legacies. But we cannot
get rid of the past or of anything that truly is ours.

The past, like a multi-rooted morning glory, blooms year
after year after year. No matter how many miles of the lateral,
interconnected root system you manage to rip out, you cannot
eradicate it entirely. Even poisoning it with weed killer doesn't
work well, because the surrounding good plants often are
killed, too.

The shadows of the past must be embraced as we work to
gather our selves together into a single whole. That task is at

the heart of true recovery and true change. According to psychotherapist Sheldon Kopp, author of *The Hanged Man,* "It is clear that the hidden forces within . . . are dangerous to him ONLY when he is unaware of them. Even the darkest of matters can shed light once they have been . . . looked at with unblinking eyes."

The nonjudgmental approach of profound self-acceptance coupled with the power of acknowledging thoughts and feelings gives us the ability to look at our past with unblinking eyes. For those in therapy where compiling a family history is recommended, the Creative Processes in this chapter provide a different way to elicit information you can use for that purpose.

For those in a Twelve-Step program, these unusual and creative exercises can assist with the searching and fearless moral inventory called for in Step Four. In addition, you will find ideas to help with both Step Eight, which advises making amends to those we have harmed, and Step Ten, which suggests taking continued personal inventory and promptly admitting wrongs.

Addictions and other diseases of denial often can be traced back to early hurt, loss, deprivation, neglect, trauma, or abuse. Sometimes these events happened to us as early as infancy, and when they remain out of awareness they can control our lives.

The following Creative Process is the most powerful way I know to reexperience the past without the help of a professional therapist. Reexperiencing the past helps you to integrate both its pain and its power. Although this process works best as a solitary exploration, it could be done with a partner functioning as a listener, a quiet witness. It's vitally important, however, that you be allowed to fully experience whatever happens without interference or interpretation, and having a witness present may create inhibitions. The hardest part of this for most people is just surrendering to the process.

There are two ways to retrieve the past. The usual way is through the door of memory, which begins: "I remember when . . . " Sigmund Freud said that there is a censor standing guard at the door of memory, which alters and distorts all that comes through that door.

Creative Process #9
Reliving the Past

Another way of retrieving the past is to go back to a time in the past to which you have an emotional connection—either positive or negative.

Pick a specific date or time of year. If you're using a tape recorder, it helps to close your eyes. Begin writing or speaking about that time in the present tense—as if it were happening right now. "It is November 22nd, 1963. I am ____years old. President Kennedy was assassinated today. I heard about it when _____." Or "Today is my ninth birthday. The date is _____, and I'm living with _____."

From there continue in the present tense, aiming for an unthinking stream-of-consciousness flow onto paper or into the tape recorder. Record the emotionally based scene as if it were happening now, moment by moment.

Don't be alarmed if you find yourself weeping or laughing or raging as you relive these scenes. There is no danger that you will become trapped in the past or evoke any emotion that you are not equipped to handle. So, resist the temptation to shut down prematurely; encourage yourself to continue to record all the details and feelings from that event. No detail is too minor, no feeling too petty to record.

Some events in our past are so sensitive and potentially painful that it may be useful to find a safe or neutral point of view from which to observe and record certain events. For instance, Valorie, who was in therapy because of an extremely abusive childhood, wanted to go back to the time her mother had beaten her so severely that she ended up in the hospital. It was not necessary for her to directly experience all that pain again, but it was desirable for her therapy to understand more about what happened.

I asked her to tell me a little bit about where the event took place. She described her tiny bedroom and the window curtains with figures of ballerinas on them. I suggested that she record what happened that day from the vantage point of one of those figures. "I am a ballerina on Valorie's curtain. Valorie is ten and a half years old. She is lying on her bed and . . ." Using an inanimate object enabled Valorie to experience what happened from a safe distance.

Another way to deal with sensitive material is to create a safe place in which to write or record this time from the past. Call a friend and ask if you can do this process at her house, especially if she knows enough not to rescue you or try to protect you from the pain of the past. The best kind of friend for this purpose is one who knows and respects that you will ask for what you need.

After you are comfortable with this process, use it even to recapture and reexperience preverbal experiences in your life. It's also possible to use this process to re-create the feelings of being in the womb and the struggle to be born. Although I suspect these ideas are a stretch for some of you, think of it as an exercise in creativity rather than something bound by your known reality.

The Creative Processes in this chapter contain many ways to come to terms with the past. They are designed to be used over a long period of time or as needed, not done compulsively one after another. Look them over to begin with so you will be familiar with the variety. The best attitude with which to approach them is one of curiosity and discovery. Do not try to control the process in any way. Do not predict, censor, or interpret. The outpourings will not be equally useful anyway; some of it is bound to be contaminated by intellectual garbage.

What I am looking for when I do any of these processes is a half-line that sheds light on the incident or illuminates in some small way the time I'm writing or talking about—the kind of half-line that evokes an "Aha, so that's what it's about!" response as I'm doing them or reviewing them later.

The following variation can help prime the pump leading to a flow or outpouring of past experiences.

Creative Process #10
Streets Where You Lived

1. Provide yourself with crayons or colored marking pens and large sheets of paper. When you're ready, plunge in and begin working without thinking about it too much. Take a few minutes to list the countries, states, cities, and neighborhoods you've lived in. List some, or all, of the street addresses at which you've lived.
2. Pick one address and a season and year you lived there, such as spring 1984. Work for five to ten minutes on a separate sheet of paper. Without worrying about doing it properly, sketch the front of the house and/or the floor plan. This has nothing to do with artistic talent. Again, without thinking, take a few minutes to sketch a view of your favorite room from the doorway.
3. How old were you when you lived there? On a separate sheet of paper, write: I am ____years old. The date is _____. The address where I live is _____. Then list the rooms in the house, the other people who live there, the family pets, the neighbors and friends you know, the stores, parks, and other familiar places in that neighborhood. Jot down whatever first comes to mind. There are no wrong answers.
4. Take another five to ten minutes to describe a special event that happened in that house. Write in the present tense, as if it were happening this moment. Aim for a stream-of-consciousness outpouring onto paper or into the recorder.

Compiling a family history, genealogy, or family tree is another valuable way to gain information and insight into family patterns and problems. As you talk to family members, the best question to ask is, "Tell me about the time. . . ." Picking a specific focus will often tap into a richer vein of stories than random reminiscences. Encourage yourself to listen patiently and to refrain from interrupting. People need to tell their stories. Your role is to facilitate their stories, not to compete by telling yours.

Photographs, snapshots, pieces of furniture, and other ordinary or treasured objects from the past can also evoke stories from family members. You could say: "Tell me what was happening around this time" or "Tell me what this thing was used for" or "How does this work?" Avoid questions that begin with *why*.

If family members are not available or are unwilling to cooperate, it's possible to use mementos and the following process as your own entryway into the past.

Creative Process #11
Images of the Past

1. Choose a snapshot taken of you during a time you want to know more about. Carefully saved childhood drawings of favorite pets or other family scenes could also be used.
2. Allow the snapshot or drawing to describe itself, using its own words. Think of yourself as taking dictation. "I am a picture of _____, and in the background I show _____. I was taken when _____ and _____. Other interesting facts about this time and place and this person include _____ and _____." Keep going for three to five minutes.
3. Choose just one element of the photo and allow it to express itself in its own words, using the same technique. "I am the image of Corky, the family cat, in the picture of _____, and I know some things about what was going on in the family at that time." Again keep going for three to five minutes. You can use as many elements in the picture, including trees, fences, and articles of clothing, as you have time and interest.

4. Now you can ask questions of the picture or any image that has expressed itself in its own voice. Record the question and then quickly, without stopping to think, record its answer. Ask it to comment on anything that may be missing from the pictured scene. Ask it to give a title to that chapter of your life. Ask it to discuss the quality of life portrayed in the photograph. For any question you can think of, it has the power to answer.

The answers come from that deep source within you that knows what happened. Everything you have ever seen, heard, touched, smelled, or experienced is recorded somewhere within you. This technique is simply another indirect-sourced way to stimulate your subconscious.

Accessing the Subconscious

The subconscious also conceals strong emotions. Whenever unusual positive or negative feelings overwhelm us or our reactions surprise us, they often are related to unresolved events or problems from the past. That door to the past often is triggered by sensory stimuli such as glimpsing fuchsia hollyhocks against a pink stucco wall, feeling the texture of a velvet dress, tasting cotton candy again, hearing a favorite melody or advertising jingle, or catching a whiff of a familiar fragrance, aroma, or odor.

Geraldine, to her dismay, found that both the faint odor of cigar smoke and the sight of anyone smoking a cigar evoked rage. "All I want to do is punch him out!" she said with fire in her eyes. Because she seldom experienced anger, much less rage, she found this overreaction disturbing.

Geraldine, whose favorite uncle had been a cigar smoker, knew that she hadn't always had an aversion to cigars. As she began to write about it in her journal, she eventually uncovered the source of the problem. Seven years earlier she had been the victim of what today would be called date-rape. The man had smoked a cigar. Both the smell and the sight of a cigar subconsciously evoked the event she'd repressed. She'd forgotten the event, but her body hadn't forgotten the feelings. But her rage didn't disappear just because she found out what triggered it. Her long-buried feelings of resentment not only had to be uncovered and acknowledged but also had to be released. Creative Process #12 is one way of releasing or neutralizing resentment.

Resentment is a familiar feeling for most of us—that churning grievance toward people for "what they did to me." Like an ugly fungus, it grows in the darkness of our minds, feeding on the moist decay of our hidden thoughts and feelings.

Many people think resentment is the same thing as rage or anger, particularly because it often begins as anger, whether conscious or unconscious. Anger, however, always occurs in the present moment. For some people that angry moment can last for hours if they're in the midst of expressing their feelings in an explosive confrontation. Often, however, extended angry feelings are fed and compounded by stored-up past resentments. The word "resentment" literally means "to feel again"; therefore, resentment is not a primary feeling, but a secondary one.

If you respond appropriately to your angry feelings when they occur, you do not walk away with resentment. But appropriate response to feeling angry does not usually mean punching people out or getting violent. According to therapist Leonard Shaw, "The expression of anger will always lead to joy, *if* you have no need to be right or get your own way." Taking care of your angry feelings could be as simple as telling the other person what you're feeling or admitting your feelings to yourself and choosing not to do anything else about them. It's denying feelings or discounting them that gives rise to resentment.

Many of us, unfortunately, are like Geraldine, so out of touch with our feelings that we don't recognize our anger until it's too late. Then we don't experience the anger, but only the resentment. The worst part about resentment is that it breeds, storing up negative energy in the confines of our minds and mortgaging our time and energy.

If you respond appropriately
to your angry feelings when they occur,
you do not walk away with resentment.

Every resentment is preceded by a moment of deferring to the other person or of holding back from effective action that may have taken care of your feelings. Effective action will neutralize the effects of whatever the person did or said or didn't do or say. So, if you can find the point at which you failed to act, then as you experience the moment when you gave away your power, resentment often disappears. You can use that knowledge to make sure that kind of thing does not happen again.

Sometimes that moment of deferral, that moment when you gave away your power, may be a long way back in time from the moment you're describing, but it is there nonetheless. Geraldine had to go back six months before the incident. She discovered that her moment of deferral came when she agreed to date a man whom she had earlier described to a friend as "too macho. I'm not sure he really thinks much of women." Her failure to act happened when, out of loneliness, she ignored her intuitive feelings about the kind of man he was and began a relationship with him anyway.

The following process is the most valuable way of dealing with negative feelings growing out of hurt, anger, blame, and rage. It will enable you to reclaim that wasted energy.

Creative Process #12
Neutralizing Resentment

Use your notebook or tape recorder.

1. Recall a persistent resentment against another person. Take a minute or two to record the circumstances of the last

encounter that triggered the old resentment. Describe the person involved and what was said and done as if you were a reporter. Include as much detail as possible.

2. Now look for that moment of nonaction or deferral, that point at which you could have done or said something that would have taken care of your feelings.

3. Whether or not you can find the moment of deferral, ask yourself, "Am I willing to let go of this resentment?" or "Am I willing to forgive this person?" or "Am I willing to release my demands of that person?" You do not have to feel forgiving; you just have to be willing to write or say the following: "I release and let go of my resentment toward _____ for _____" and "I release and let go of my resentment toward myself for _____." Or, "I forgive _____ for _____" and "I forgive myself for _____." Fill in the blanks with the name of the person and the transgression, and your name and whatever your part in the transaction was. Repeat one version of these twin releasing statements until you have worked through all aspects of the resentment.

It is essential that you do this as a twin releasing process: every statement about the other person must be followed by a statement releasing or forgiving yourself. The most valuable information often comes when you state what you are forgiving yourself for. By the way, this has nothing to do with religious notions about forgiveness and will work even if you use harsh language to describe yourself and the other person involved.

When Geraldine forgave herself for "letting my loneliness overcome my better judgment," she healed the rage and buried resentment that had been controlling her life.

4. If you find you're not willing to let go of the resentment, then notice what objections you have to doing this exercise. Consider what it does for you to hold onto this resentment. Does it justify some thoughts or behavior toward the person or make you feel better about a failure of yours?

Hannah, for instance, was involved in a messy lawsuit and found herself unwilling to use the releasing process on her soon-to-be ex-business partner, even though the resentment was hurting her. She finally realized that she felt she wouldn't get a good legal settlement if she released or forgave him, so hanging onto the resentment made a kind of sense.

Remember that the purpose of the exercise is to free your energy, not to condone anyone else's behavior or even to let the other person off the hook. The purpose is to let *you* off the hook, to release you from the bondage of the past. Therefore, after you've used this process for a while, you may prefer to go immediately to the twin releasing part when you are feeling resentful.

Caution: This process is to be used only for freeing yourself from the hard feelings and negativity created by blame and resentment. It is not used to forgive someone face to face, unless that person has specifically requested it. Not only is it arrogant to forgive someone in person without permission, but also it can be perceived as an act of hostility.

You may have to repeat this powerful process many times, especially with important relationships or long-standing resentments or grievances. Novelist James Hilton said, "If you forgive people enough you belong to them, and they to you, whether either person likes it or not—squatter's rights of the heart." You can heal important relationships, even without access to the other people involved, if you're willing to do the repeated hard work this resentment neutralizing process entails.

Other Secondary Feelings

Resentment is not the only secondary feeling. Just as the secondary feeling of resentment is warmed over from the primary feeling of anger, so anxiety is warmed over from the primary feeling of fear. True fear is a here-and-now feeling, a momentary response to a perceived threatening stimulus. If I'm out for a walk and see a rattlesnake coiled and ready to strike in front of me, I'm going to feel fearful; the adrenaline rush and rapid heartbeat enable me to react and save myself. Stimulus—the rattlesnake; response—fear. Anxiety, on the other hand, feeds on self-stimulated thoughts. If a week after the rattlesnake scare I'm walking down the same path and remember what happened, I may get an adrenaline rush and rapid heartbeat the same as I did before; it feels like fear to me. However, there is no real danger; my anxiety is clearly being stimulated by my own thoughts.

Even the feeling of joy has its secondary counterpart: nostalgia—that longing for "the good old days." Another primary feeling, grief, can slide into self-pity, which is nothing more than warmed-over grief. Grief, however, is a cyclical process rather than a momentary response to a loss. It is possible to tell the difference between the two; if you interrupt a grieving person, the person becomes bewildered, then returns to grieving. Interrupting self-pity evokes anger.

For instance, I was telling my daughter on the phone how deeply I was still grieving months after the suicide of my friend Neil. I value Deborah because she always tells me the truth, but I was shocked when she said, "Sounds to me like you're feeling sorry for yourself." Angry, I hung up on her. Then I thought about what she had said and realized she was right. I called her back and acknowledged that if I'd been really grieving, I wouldn't have felt so angry with her.

Most of these secondary or warmed-over feelings happen when there isn't anything better to do; perhaps these kinds of feelings are simply the results of boredom. Knowing about the difference between primary and secondary feelings can help you to sort out the clutter of feelings and to know which are worth your time and attention. Resentment, anxiety, self-pity, and even nostalgia are energy drains and reinforce passivity by preoccupying us so we avoid responsible action.

Resentment is warmed-over anger.
Anxiety is warmed-over fear.
Self-pity is nothing more than warmed-over grief.
Warmed-over feelings happen when there isn't
anything better to do.

Here's an active process to help clean up incomplete transactions from the past.

Creative Process #13
Appreciating the Past

Use your notebook or tape recorder. If you're using the recorder, read through the steps, then name the person and do the other steps before going on to the next person. Otherwise:

1. List twelve important or memorable people in your life. They can be living and present, or absent, or even dead.
2. List one or more things you learned from each of them. What beliefs did each person teach you? Check the quiz on Beliefs in chapter four for statements you marked as true. What skills did you learn? What habits did you learn? List good and bad things, big and little things. Here are some examples: "Men are no damn good" or "Women—you can't live with them; you can't live without them." Tree-climbing or kite-flying; saying "please" and "thank you"; baking an angel food cake; being sarcastic; making your bed every morning; "obey authority" or "challenge authority"; playing martyr; "Every cloud has a silver-lining"; the Puritan work ethic. And so on.
3. Go back over your list. Decide whether you feel appreciation, or resentment, or both toward that person for each thing you learned.
4. This is the action step. Decide which ones you are willing to write notes of appreciation for, whether or not you send them. Decide which ones you're willing to do the resentment releasing process on. Do them.

Clearing away old business from the past and completing failed or unexpressed communications is like a spring cleaning of mental and emotional closets. It frees up time and energy to use today.

Hannah, however, felt a lack of completion after she wrote a letter of appreciation to her dead husband. She found that, to feel complete, she needed to put it in an envelope with his first name on it, but without a stamp or return address, and actually deposit it in a mailbox. Use your creativity to devise symbolic ways to complete old business with those who are deceased or unavailable.

Writing letters to your mother and father (even if they aren't available now), can be a worthwhile and satisfying way to deal with old hurts, regrets, and disappointments. Sarah's recovery depended on her coming to terms with her feelings about her mother, accepting the traits and behaviors she shared with the mother she had scorned and having that be okay, and understanding the ways she was different from her mother. Making peace with our parents, or our lack of parents, enables us to get on with our lives.

Our parents and our children serve as distorted reflections of the traits we like about ourselves as well as those we've tried to change. When my four grown children get together and one of them does something that reminds them of their father or me, one of them is bound to singsong, "Little Moms and little Dads!" There's more than a trace of irony in their teasing, because it's often the behavior they've objected most strenuously to that they find themselves acting out.

I often look at my daughter as well as my sons and see myself reflected. They are all fiercely independent and irreverent, and they all challenge authority. They also are highly creative, forthright, and hard workers with entrepreneurial spirits. They are not easy to live with, but they are always interesting.

These reflections of ourselves are neverending, because every person we admire, as well as those we detest, reflects some trait, prejudice, or opinion about us. We cannot love or hate anything in someone else that is not also a part of who we are. According to diarist Anais Nin, "We don't see things as they are, we see them as we are."

When you see generosity in the people you know and those you meet, or when you perceive dishonesty, or stupidity, or loyalty, or creativity, all that perception does is hold a mirror for you to look into, if you're willing. You can use that knowledge, when you stop reacting to it, to help gather yourself into a single whole.

Here's an interesting process to help you peer into other mirrors in your life.

Creative Process #14
Reflecting Mirrors

1. List the people in your life who serve as mirrors for you. Elaina's list: "Auntie Jo, my daughter, my best friend Gwen, my boss, my father, my first husband, his mother, and cousin Hugh."
2. List the actual mirrors in your life. Fred found five: "My bathroom mirror, the mirrors in my Chevy, the mirror over the chest of drawers in the bedroom, a wooden hand mirror that belonged to my mother, and the mirror in the men's room at work."
3. List the other mirrors—those things that reflect your personality in your life. Jane's list: "bills and credit cards, drawers of makeup, closets of clothes I seldom wear, my Cuisinart, and Janie's rainbow kite." Aaron listed, "Smoky—the rocking wooden dragon I built, my set of fine Japanese chisels, my pickup truck, and my faded green flannel shirt."
4. Discuss your relationship with the other mirrors in your life. Comment on what each person, place, or thing reflects about you. Jane wrote, "My mirrors show that I'm impulsive and really enjoy the moment, but don't like paying for yesterday's pleasures."

5. Pick one item (or more) from the second or third list and allow it to speak in its own voice to tell you more about itself—and therefore about you. Feel free to ask it questions. Fred's bathroom mirror commented that it had been a lot happier with what it saw every morning since Fred quit drinking. Fred asked it, "What do you think I should do about the complaints that I'm always late for work?" and it replied, "If your paycheck was doubled whenever you were on time for a whole month, how often do you think you'd be late?"

Food for Thought

Remember, these end-of-chapter questions can be playfully or thoughtfully considered and then released. They don't need answers.

- Are you willing to return again and again to weep your unshed tears?
- Are you ready to gather your whole life into a single whole?
- Are you willing to feel all your emotions past and present?
- Are you ready to release your resentments so you can reclaim your energy and take back your power?

· III ·
Creativity,
Joy,
and Well-being

·8·

Creativity versus Recovery

Any psychiatrist will tell you that making a basket, or making a horseshoe, or giving anything form gives you a confidence in the universe . . . that it has form, see. When you talk about your troubles and go to somebody about them, you're just a fool. The best way to settle them is to make something that has form, because all you want to do is get a sense of form. ROBERT FROST

E VERYBODY has creative energy, and everybody uses it in some way. I'm not talking only about participation in the obvious creative arts such as music, drama, poetry, dance, writing, and painting, although involvement with any of these certainly requires creative energy. Creative energy is that force which makes a difference and gets things done, and often in a new or different way. What are you spending your creative energy on?

Creativity also has been defined as the cross on which you bare your soul; therefore, any involvement with the creative process offers catharsis, a way to settle your troubles. Using your doubt, pain, anxieties, and death as energy to create with gives you a chance to get a sense of form, a sense of purpose for your life. The essential wisdom of the creative process is the opportunity it presents to use everything that has ever happened to you, or ever will happen, in a kind of death-defying act.

A woman named Elizabeth Layton, for instance, fought a losing battle with depression for most of her adult life. At the age of sixty-eight she took a drawing class, hoping to find something to do. What she found was "a mission," and her allegorical drawings not only have been widely exhibited but also have served as a testimony to her recovery from depression. The multitude of recovery issues as well as the excesses of addictions should be appreciated as creative gifts disguised as problems.

As people begin to discover their true character, to unconditionally accept what they find and embrace the confusion of the world and the shadows of the past, the similarities between people in recovery and creative people become more apparent. According to psychologist Carl Rogers, "The mainspring of creativity appears to be the same tendency which we discover so deeply as the curative force in psychotherapy . . . the urge to expand, extend, develop, mature." He suggests that although this tendency may "be hidden behind elaborate facades which deny its existence . . . it exists in every individual and awaits only the proper conditions to be released and expressed."

Society and Creative People

Unfortunately, our society often discourages the proper conditions for creativity. Creativity thrives on fantasy, reflection, humor, and playfulness. Our culture maintains that those activities are a waste of time and that people who exhibit those traits are immature, lazy, or even insane. Society's other blocks to creativity include the attitude that reason, logic, utility, and practicality are good while feelings, intuition, qualitative judgments, and pleasure are bad.

Our society considers problem solving to be serious business. Playfulness is for children only. Problems, like drug addiction, must be solved only by scientific thinking and lots of money. Even though that approach clearly hasn't worked, traditional wisdom is preferred over innovative ideas. Creative expression and the creative individual are esteemed only when validated by the marketplace. Money, prestige, or power determine worth; unless the price tag is visible, there's little perceived value.

Those celebrated materialistic values of our society send a loud negative message to the creative artist, the misfit, the innovator, the independent thinker. Creative people who stretch boundaries, who exhibit childlike delight, who get impatient with rigidified systems, are crowded to the fringes of society. In addition, those mavericks who place everything else above chasing money and accumulating things are considered socially suspect.

"Creative people are especially observant," said Frank Barron in *Scientific American*:

> They often express part-truths, but this they do vividly; the part they express is the generally unrecognized. . . . They are thus independent . . . and will suffer great personal pain to testify correctly. Their universe is more complex, and in addition they usually lead more complex lives, seeking tension in the interest of the pleasure they obtain upon its discharge. They have more contact than most people do with the life of the unconscious, with fantasy, reverie, the world of imagination.
>
> The creative person is both more primitive and more cultured, more destructive and more constructive, crazier and saner, than the average person.

Much of the above description of the creative person, especially the last sentence, applies equally to the addictive personality and the person in recovery. Our culture considers these extremes to be dangerous. Addicts who have turned to drugs or alcohol to resist the pain of living in society become prisoners of their own resistance. Artists resist society by separating themselves from it; then they often produce works that provoke controversy and shake up the establishment. Truly creative people neither fit neatly into the structures nor live happily with the strictures of society.

Artists or Addicts?

Creativity tends to lie dormant in an atmosphere where naked-ness is risky. The nakedness of self-exposure is always risky, especially because artists tend to be oversensitive and to over-react according to normal societal standards. But for both artists and the addictive personality, the fear of exposure is often mingled with a desire for attention. The addictive per-son doesn't get attention in positive ways, but gets that atten-tion by getting sick or getting into trouble of one sort or another. Both creative expression and addiction are attempts to control our experiences, to bring order out of chaos, to give form to our lives, to control our pain. Recovery, too, is a re-sponse to pain.

Creativity, however, transmutes pain. Creativity, like true recovery, demands surrender. The challenges of recovery, and all the steps to recovery, are designed to facilitate that surren-der. The pain and chaos are transmuted by surrendering to them, wandering around in them, and emerging out the other side. I suspect there's a higher incidence of creative potential in addictive personalities. Maybe those persons with so-called addictive personalities are just at odds with their real selves, their creative selves, because they're busy trying to live the way that society says they should instead of the way that would satisfy them.

If you are currently in recovery, your challenge is to find the right constructive and creative outlet for your pain and to turn your recovery into a creative act. All truly creative acts are acts of self-exposure, but so is recovery. All communication, if it is honest, feels risky, but so does recovery. All creative acts are scary, but so is recovery. People in recovery instinctively know these things. Any resistance you've had to doing some of the self-discovery Creative Processes probably comes from the fear of self-exposure, or of knowing what you know. Most blocks to creativity come from that same fear.

The Fear of Creativity

"Emotional blocks," James Adams warned in *Conceptual Block-busting,* may "prevent us from communicating ideas to others in a manner which will gain them acceptance." Emotional blocks to creativity, to risk-taking, and to recovery include fear of making a mistake, fear of failure, and an overriding desire for security and order—"no appetite for chaos." These barriers to growth plague both creative people and people in recovery, interfering with their ability to effectively use their creative energies.

The Creative Processes in this book, the process of recovery itself, and the process of creating a painting or a song or a short story all require and use the same personal resources. If you already have or can find the best form of artistic or creative expression for yourself, you may not want or need to do the other processes in this book. You must be willing, however, to pay the price for making that creative activity a high priority. True artistic or creative expression will demand much from you and will use all your experience and all your pain. It is physically, mentally, emotionally, and spiritually demanding work, and it also requires a healthy life-style.

According to a *Parade* magazine article, for the first few years people in recovery keep going with the support and encouragement of others. After that point, passion for their work, especially when it involves the creative process in some way, is the most important link to participating fully in life again. Actor Tony Curtis, interviewed about his involvement with painting, said, "My recovery has nothing to do with alcohol or drugs now; it has to do with recovering as a human being." An artist's completion, or satisfaction, often is in the art rather than in society. Certainly creativity offers a constructive outlet for the energy of people in recovery who seek excitement. If you are in recovery from an addiction, obsession, or compulsion, you may already know how to live as an artist—on the fringes of society.

I'm suggesting that if you can't or don't fit well into society, you view that as an advantage, not a liability, and find a constructive outlet for those outlaw or maverick tendencies. If the rules of society don't make any sense to you, find a way to create an alternative. That's what artists do, whether they create new universes by writing science fiction and fantasy, or paint their visions on canvas, or sculpt in wire and clay. Much that is called art is subversive. Creative expression is about *not* following rules. It's about digging into yourself and finding your truths and giving form to them.

If you are in recovery, it may be useful to begin to see yourself as a latent artist rather than as a self-destructive juvenile. In addition, if you survive the long apprenticeship to art and become commercially successful, your having a history of addiction or other difficulty will be seen not as a terrible thing but as having a colorful past. However, you must be prepared for the possibility that the people in your life who objected to your self-destructive pursuits may also object, perhaps in less vocal ways, to your creative involvement. The creative arts require the same kind of energy and commitment that relationships do.

Creative Involvement

Creative involvement, however, does not require so-called talent or have anything to do with taking lessons on how to do it right. Creativity means using everything that you are— your intelligence and your experience—in a natural and spontaneous expression. Creative involvement may require a sense of apprenticeship; apprenticeship begins with involvement. What's also required is an honest desire or interest and the willingness to plunge in and teach yourself what you need to know by doing it. I'm not talking about perfection or perfectionism, but crude vitality and common passion.

Eric Hoffer, the longshoreman-philosopher, said, "I am a common man and proud of my commonness. But talent is common too—it's all around us, only most of the time it gets wasted." It gets wasted because too often people think that it requires credentials or permission from someone or something outside themselves to exercise that talent. A teacher is simply one who teaches, not just a person who has a college degree. Craftspeople who love their work are artists even if nobody else ever sees or validates their work. It's not the opinion or sanction of others, but our own authentic expression that we must validate for ourselves.

If you want to be an artist, you do what artists do. Artists don't set out to create ART, they set aside some time, then they show up and get involved with the materials and tools of their medium. Artist Frederick Franck warned, "A drawing is not a thing but an act. If a drawing succeeds, be happy but don't congratulate yourself. If it is a miss, don't grieve over it but take a new sheet of paper."

Here's a process that can help you find your form of artistic or creative expression, if you don't already have one.

Creative Process #15
What's Your Pleasure?

1. Buy, beg, or borrow any of the following:
   - A large box of colored crayons or chalk (pastels) and a pad of newsprint; or a sketch pad and drawing pencils; or a simple snapshot camera and film; or a video camera and blank cassette; or an audio recorder and blank cassette.
   - A 150-page spiral notebook and a comfortable pen.
   - Three beanbags or balls for juggling, or favorite music to dance to.
   - An inexpensive harmonica, guitar, or other musical instrument.

- A good pocketknife and a variety of woods to carve or whittle; or fabric, yarn, and needles for a fiber art project.
2. Spend at least an hour every day actively involved with your choice of materials. Do something; don't think about it; don't worry about how to do it or where to start. Just play with it; pretend you're an artist. Better yet, pretend you're a ten-year-old pretending you're an artist! The emphasis is on process, not product, on pleasure, not work.
3. With your first choice, continue your active creative involvement for three weeks to three months. Avoid expectations of any kind. Be careful about telling anyone what you're doing. If your interest in your first choice expands, explore further by using different materials. Or, try another idea from the list if it appeals to you.
4. Eventually, you could use your chosen art to make an informal documentary of your childhood, your neighborhood, your recovery, your anger, or your life.

The Healing Power of Creativity

The arts are healing. Whether you're moving your body in dance, mime, or juggling; making music; creating or capturing visual images; working in wood or fabric; or pouring words onto paper, the involvement can take you out of yourself in a therapeutic way. When you surrender to the medium and the creative idea, you lose your ego self.

Aaron's creation of colorful rocking animals helped him to nurture the neglected child within himself. Jane wrote fairy tales for the abandoned Janie within her. Fred, trying to stay sober, started sketching street people, dark tavern scenes, and other glimpses of Skid Row; Carla, a former drug addict, used drug paraphernalia to make striking collages. Both Fred's and Carla's work was later used in a community awareness program.

A Hearst News Service feature told about Frankcina Glass,

a teenage black girl from Atlanta. "Stories would come to me," she said. "And they got longer and longer, and they got drawed out so much in my head that I had to put them down on paper to get rid of them." As Frankcina began writing what her mind dictated, she found a new kind of therapy: "When I wrote, I forgot everything. When I got mad, writing calmed me down."

People need to tell their stories, whether verbally in support groups or among friends, or in words on paper. According to a 1985 study at Southern Methodist University, people who wrote or talked about traumatic experiences were significantly healthier physically than those who kept those experiences to themselves. "I create, so I don't destroy," explained one novelist in a television interview.

Not too long ago a young woman called me, looking for a ghostwriter to help her write a book. She was newly married, but had been involved with the underworld for the previous seven years. "I want it written down because I need to get it out of my body. It's like a disease; I need to get it out of my system." She instinctively understood that her recovery from her past depended on telling her story. She was willing to risk self-exposure out of the need to heal herself.

People need to tell their stories.

All writing is an act of self-exposure. Most writers' blocks arise out of that emotional fear of self-exposure. If writers are not sometimes terrified by the potential for revealing themselves in their work, they simply do not understand the nature of the creative process. If creative artists do not have a sense of risk or fear of exposure as they work, chances are they are not digging deep enough within themselves to make what they're doing worthwhile.

In addition, creative or artistic expression can use compulsive, obsessive, addictive energy in a constructive way. Fiction writing in particular can use much of the fantasizing and rationalizing expertise that many of those in recovery have accumulated. The need for high drama, stimulation, and intensity can also be absorbed in storytelling.

Here's a way to help you start telling your stories:

Creative Process #16
Once Upon a Time

Pick a memorable incident from your life or from the life of someone you have known. Begin writing a story—an adventure story or a fairy tale. Start with "Once upon a time. . . ." If it's from your life, pick another name for the main character. Write steadily, without thinking, without stopping, without being bound by the reality of the original incident. Finish it in the way you would have liked it to work out.

Here's Jane's story about Freeing-the-Princess:

> Once upon a time an ordinary princess fidgeted in the tower, waiting for a handsome prince to rescue her. She'd been waiting a long time in her room overlooking the rose garden. Queen Patience and King Loyal had often told her that her prince would come, and that this was the way the world worked. "All you have to do is be good," said her father. "And beautiful," said her mother.
>
> So the ordinary princess tried very hard to be good and to be beautiful. Every day roses from the garden appeared in her tower room. One day as she was combing her ordinary brown hair a dreadful thought occurred to her. What if her parents were wrong about the way the world worked? What if she wasn't good enough? What if she couldn't be beautiful enough?
>
> Although the questions unsettled her, they sparked exciting speculations. What if there were other possibilities? What would happen if she stopped waiting and came down from the tower? What would happen if she picked her own roses from the castle garden?
>
> The ordinary princess tried the door of her tower room and was surprised to find it unlocked. She ran down the stairs and strolled into the garden. Her parents looked shocked.

The ordinary princess looked happy, a radiant smile beautifying her face.

Creating this story helped Jane to see how long and in how many ways she had imprisoned herself and had given away her power. (Reclaiming your power through brainstorming creative solutions for your problems can also be useful.)

The difficulties that face both the creative artist and the person in recovery are similar. They both must find the proper balance between encouraging a healthy self-esteem and reducing that part of the ego that rules as a tyrannical godlike king. Another necessity for artists and addicts is the importance of killing Pollyanna, of overcoming that curse of niceness that discourages truth and authenticity. Telling the truth and being authentic are necessary to encourage creative energy.

Creative Energy

The creative energy of Bill Wilson founded Alcoholics Anonymous and assured his recovery; the creative energy of Candy Lightner, grieving over the death of her daughter, established MADD—Mothers Against Drunk Drivers. One of my students who was victimized by a quasi-therapeutic cult not only writes consumer awareness articles on the subject but also founded an organization to help other victims. Her creative energy that goes into the organization also helps to heal her recovery issues.

Both creative acts and creative arts use creative energies. Both creative acts and creative arts facilitate recovery, because the creative energy is flowing in a positive direction. Even if the original impetus to act comes from a negative event, the goal and the result are positive.

One interesting fact I've observed about my workshops is that people usually come in search of something positive. They want to learn to write, to keep a journal, to expand their creativity. Because their desire is positive they're likely to learn more, including more about themselves and their recovery issues, than if they had come to get rid of something or to fix themselves. In the act of creating they learn that the stuff they need to create with is within themselves.

The first task for the aspiring creative artist is self-knowledge. Self-knowledge is the result of creative efforts, especially failed efforts. The two things feed each other in a wondrous dance.

At the Center of Arts Therapy in New York City, people with serious mental disorders are encouraged to become involved with art, or music, or writing as a way of getting outside themselves, of expressing feeling, of transcending their pain. One man involved in music therapy talked about being "in tune" and feeling alive.

The difference between the working mode and the creative mode is like the difference between prayer and meditation; prayer is a talking to God; meditation is a quiet listening, the opening of your heart to allow guidance to emerge, to flow into and through you.

In the creative mode there is no sense of pushing, shoving, striving, or making things happen. You know you're in it when your experience of what you're doing is fun, enjoyable, or pleasurable; when you get lost in what you're doing; when you feel no separation between yourself and what you're doing; when the judging or evaluating part of you is quiet and there's no sense of needing to perform. Your attitude is permissive—anything goes. There are no specifications, no parameters, no boundaries, no guidelines, only glorious possibilities; the question of whether you're really being creative does not even arise. As a matter of fact, if you ask yourself that question, the answer will be no.

The Necessity to Create

People create for reasons of inner drive, whether it be for purposes of conflict resolution, recovery, self-fulfillment, or all three. People also create for other reasons, such as fame or fortune.

At least part of creativity, however, occurs in an area of the mind below the conscious level. Creativity and neuroses may stem from the same source; the physical manifestations of both creative excitement and anxiety are the same.

Although creativity can provoke anxiety attacks, creative expression is essential for the fully functioning personality. What creative expression have you chosen? What other creative interests have you recognized that are worth further exploration? For more ideas, check the noncredit classes and workshops of your local colleges and facilities that offer adult education.

Whatever you choose, it's best to see your involvement not as a frivolous hobby or pastime or as time-wasting something-to-do. Your creative expression also should not be seen as therapy or a recovery tactic; neither should you think of it as a vocation or a profession or a money-maker.

Said psychologist Teresa Amabile,

> It is bad to be in a situation where reward is the focus of what you do. The key to creativity is to concentrate while you're working on a task on what is enjoyable about it, what is intrinsically satisfying. Don't think about consequences and evaluations until the job is done.
>
> Choosing the creative path means abandoning the pursuit of money, prestige, and power; but after mastery, those results may be obtained.

Even if you aspire eventually to become professional in your creative outlet or to share what you're doing with the world, take time to develop yourself in private. Wait for at least five years before you show anyone what you're doing. The value for you is in the doing; the emphasis needs to be on creative involvement as an outward expression of your true character, your passion. Becoming a professional with your creative expression prematurely can kill its usefulness. All paintings need not be exhibited or all stories and poems published to be worthy of the time and effort that went into them. Creative expression such as painting, gardening, writing stories or poems, even dancing, can serve a higher purpose. When

Hannah took up tap dancing at the age of sixty-two, it inspired her younger friends to think of activating some of their old dreams.

Anais Nin spoke about creative involvement.

You must not fear, hold back, count or be a miser with your thoughts or feelings. . . . Permit yourself to flow and overflow, allow for the rise in temperature, all the expansions and intensifications. Something is always born of excess: great art was born of great terrors, great loneliness, great inhibitions, instabilities, and it always balances them.

The challenge inherent in all our excesses, difficulties, problems, and addictions is to create ways to use everything we are and everything that happens for our own education and enlightenment.

Food for Thought

Here are some questions to stimulate your creativity:

- What are you spending your creative energy on?
- What are you making or giving form to?
- What are you doing that gives you confidence in the universe?
- What are you creating that gives you confidence in yourself?
- Are you using your troubles as potential creative energy?
- Are you finding new and constructive ways to channel your creative energies?
- Are you enjoying your creative involvement?

·9·

Well-Being—
A Do-It-Yourself
Project

We are very externally oriented—toward things, money, achievement, position—and anyone who is introspectively oriented is suspect. . . . How distrustful our culture is of looking internally, of knowing thyself. Lack of self-knowledge is perhaps one of the major and most profound causes of many diseases. KENNETH PELLETIER

EALTH and well-being flow from the ongoing process of embracing the shadows of the past as they emerge, of utilizing them for growth, of being truthful with ourselves about what we're feeling right now, and of finding creative and constructive ways to handle plans and dreams of the future. These ongoing actions reflect a commitment to well-being and self-knowledge.

But commitment is something that can be measured only in retrospect. I need only look at what I spend my time and energy on today to evaluate what I'm committed to. A commitment to well-being and self-knowledge is the best insurance plan to provide ongoing health benefits. Health-minded people take responsibility for their own recovery and well-being.

A higher survival rate was reported in patients who attributed their heart attacks to their own behavior rather than to "stress," chance, or the actions of others. "Patients who perceived some value in the experience of having a heart attack tended not to have a second one," said Glenn Affleck, a University of Connecticut medical psychologist. They also lived longer and stayed in better health if they avoided the inclination to blame themselves or other people.

Those who blamed the initial attack on others had a greater incidence of subsequent attacks. Patients who attributed the attack to external sources of stress were likelier to suffer a fatal heart attack. Affleck observed, however, that well-intentioned attempts to manipulate the beliefs of heart attack victims can backfire. There also seems to be a fine line between taking responsibility for what happens and avoiding subtle self-blame. "Taking responsibility for one's life can be a painful process, and there is often major resistance," Affleck said.

The repeated focus on addiction as an illness reinforces resistance to taking responsibility and does not always help people recover. If your attention remains focused on the problem, disease, or difficulty, then you are that problem, disease, or difficulty. Negative-based recovery results in overidentification with the problem and the possibility of getting stuck in recovery.

The Issue of Responsibility

The current disease-model for alcoholism and other addictions tends to reinforce helplessness, to make recovery the province of recovery professionals, and to weaken the idea of personal choice. Seeing alcoholics and others in recovery as helpless, as people who cannot take control of their lives is to ignore the issue of responsibility. The acceptance of personal responsibility always results in natural improvement.

The phenomenon of spontaneous recovery or remission from serious illnesses, including addictions, has long been part of the history of recovery; many persons who recover or change do so on their own. Responsible recovery professionals are aware of this phenomenon and encourage clients to recognize this potential for healthy choice and recovery in themselves.

Taking responsibility for our illnesses and physical difficulties does not mean blaming ourselves. Nor does it mean fantasizing that what happened is punishment or divine retribution for bad behavior.

There is, however, a law of cause and effect, and there are certain negative consequences that result from some kinds of behavior. Jane, for instance, realized that the consequences of failing to practice safe sex were not only the risk of AIDS and other sexually transmitted diseases but also a loss of trust in herself. Any sense of punishment she may experience, then, would be the effect of guilt or diminished self-esteem, which always erodes one's quality of life. Her attitude toward her behavior affected her enjoyment of the good things.

The Body-Mind Connection

Studies in the body-mind connection suggests one's attitude toward recovery dramatically affects the progress of physical rehabilitation. Cancer researchers have begun to link several personality traits with an increased susceptibility to cancer. Suppression of anger, a self-effacing need to please others, and a general lack of self-esteem characterize what is called the Type C personality. Evidently, Pollyanna pays a high price for compulsive niceness.

In the early 1980s Lydia Temoshok, a psychologist at the University of California in San Francisco, performed psychological assessments of 150 cancer (melanoma) patients. Her findings showed that many of these patients did not express negative emotions; even in the face of cancer they maintained an even temperament, almost never giving vent to anger, sadness, or fear. The patients with these Type C patterns tended to relapse more often and more severely than others. Temo-shok believes the Type C personality experiences negative feel-ings, but does not express them. Those who expressed emo-tion more openly were often found to have less aggressive tumor growth and stronger immunologic response.

In addition, positive mental states also seem to bear favor-ably on health and longevity. A factor called "joy," meaning mental resilience and vigor, was the second strongest predictor of survival time for a group of patients with recurrent breast cancer.

Another ten-year study recently concluded that cancer pa-tients who obtain emotional and social support through group therapy may survive up to twice as long as those only on medi-cal treatment. Twelve-Step and other self-help groups provide that kind of support for their members and no doubt contrib-ute to increased survival. Length of survival, however, may not be the most important issue.

On a recent talk show featuring cancer survivors, one guest loudly blamed her former husband for everything wrong in her life, including her cancer. Was her rage keeping her alive or making her sick? Where was her joy in surviving cancer and where was her sense of well-being?

"Illnesses at any time of life should not be merely cured," said Irene Claremont de Castillejo, "but utilized for growth." My secretary, Katy, who needed a hysterectomy, decided to participate fully in the experience of surgery. She learned as much as possible about her condition, then discussed surgical options with her physician. In addition, she arranged for a hypnotist to function as her anesthesiologist. Her attitude was one of total acceptance and intense interest in all the proceedings.

During the operation she was able to help stop the bleeding at the suggestion of the hypnotist, and her recovery was un-usually speedy. Katy turned her potentially traumatic bout of major surgery into a peak experience.

You don't need to emulate Katy, but to be true to your-self in using these principles. For instance, I understand that there's possibly a body-mind connection between my having the flu and other stressful things happening in my life. It can be useful for me to explore my thoughts and feelings to find the reason. Sometimes I'm just weary, and it can be more useful to decide that I have the flu because people in the office have been coughing on me. Instead of subjecting myself to a third-degree over the whys and wherefores of my condition, I just blame circumstances. Sometimes it's best to accept that both things may be true; one belief does not preclude the other. This saves me from obsessing about causes.

Here's a process to help you get the most value and potential for growth from the illnesses, accidents, *and* healthy systems that involve your physical body.

Creative Process #17
Where Does It Hurt?

1. Write down your past and present physical symptoms, diseases, addictions, aches and pains, sensitivities and allergies, illnesses, chronic conditions, and areas of tension. Add dental problems along with medical ones.
2. Are you accident-prone? Are there certain areas of your body that are injured again and again? Do you often twist your ankles, stub your toes, bite your fingernails, bark your shins, skin your knuckles, or hit your funny bone? Jot down your favorite examples.
3. Make a similar list of all the physical organs, systems, and areas of your body that are healthy, vigorous, and function efficiently; the ones that seldom give you trouble, the ones that give you pleasure, the ones that usually heal quickly.
4. Sketch a picture of your body using crayons or colored pens and drawing paper. Do not think it out, just start making marks on the paper. No prizes for art are being given here. Pretend you're a third grader and this is FUN! Stop after three minutes, even if you're not finished.
5. Pick an example from one of the first two lists (in #1 or #2)

and, on your drawing, take one minute to draw its color and shape and size in its approximate location.

6. Without thinking about it or censoring what pops into your mind, give the drawing a title—a word or a phrase that says something about what's there.

7. Allow the whole drawing or just the physical focus of it to express itself in its own words. Use the tape recorder or notebook. Aim for the stream-of-consciousness flow. Allow it to describe itself, to note what's emphasized and what's missing, to say what it's afraid of, and to say what it likes about itself.

8. Ask it questions such as "How are you feeling?" and "What or who is responsible for your condition?" If you find that another person's name comes up, seek to uncover the hard feelings that you may be holding against that person. Use the resentment-releasing process from chapter seven.

   Other questions to ask include "What are you keeping me from doing?" and "Is there another part of me that doesn't want to have to do that?" Record its answers. Ask it for clarification and advice, or use it to check out the advice you're getting from others. Ask it "Have I done everything I could to take care of you medically?" or "What would you like me to do for you now?"

9. Pick any item from the third list. Allow it to express itself. Record a discussion between the two about what they think you should do to increase your well-being. Ask them questions and record their responses. Finish up with, "What words of wisdom do you have for me at this time?" and record what they say.

The Importance of Paying Attention

The principles that operate in Creative Process #17 include the following: Whatever you pay attention to automatically begins to change, and every circumstance of our lives has a message for us in it.

When you become more familiar with this technique to obtain information about areas of physical difficulty, you can use it immediately whenever something happens. For instance, in earlier years I frequently twisted or sprained my ankles. As I began to widen my use of the stream-of-consciousness projection technique, I began using it to find out what was causing the problem. "I am Jean's sprained left ankle," I'd begin and let it express itself. I eventually found that its messages were simple things like, "Slow down; stop rushing about" or "Look before you leap; pay attention."

The more information I got, the more I paid attention to the messages and the less frequently I injured my ankles. I was free of ankle injuries for almost five years. The latest time it happened was when I'd just returned from a business trip; I'd driven three thousand miles in three weeks by myself, including visiting with a cousin about my age dying of cancer.

I knew I was fatigued so I was trying to take it easy, spending a quiet day with a friend wandering around a boat show. I was wearing good walking shoes and everything was fine, when suddenly I stumbled and heard my ankle crack as I tumbled to the ground. I sat there, crying, as my friend brought the car around. Never had I experienced such pain from an ankle injury. As I waited for the X-rays, my foot elevated and packed in ice, tears streamed down my face. Crying was not a normal reaction to this kind of thing for me, but I just couldn't stop.

I focused my attention on the injured ankle and asked the question: "What is this all about?" The answer was immediate: I needed to grieve for my cousin who had just died, but because I'd denied the pain of losing him, my ankle had provided a sharp reminder. I stopped trying to control myself and let myself sob it out. The most interesting part of the incident was how quickly the ankle healed: it obviously had already served its purpose.

***Whatever you pay attention to
automatically begins to change.***

Addiction to Pain

"The only antidote to mental suffering is physical pain," said the German philosopher Karl Marx. Whether or not you believe that, it's a provocative idea and one that presumes a body-mind connection. Recovery specialists also have observed that in a conflict between the body and the mind (or will), the body always wins. That's one of the reasons physical addictions are so powerful.

Back specialist Maggie Lettvin in *Maggie's Back Book* warned,

> Pain is a danger signal. Do not ignore it. Recognize and deal with it immediately. Watch out! There are some of you who will have become attached to that ache and will allow it as a constant companion! The luxury of staying ill, of being pitied, of being cared for, is frightening. Guard against it.

This kind of attachment can happen for those in Twelve-Step programs who over-identify with the disease model; as long as they are convinced they can never recover from their addictions, that belief will color their reality and will preclude the possibility of true change.

It's important to honor your body, to pay attention to its signals, to provide for its needs. Health and well-being basics include nonpolluted air, clean water, good food, sleep, relaxation, and exercise. You must determine your other specific needs. For instance, I've learned that for me fatigue is a depressant, and I need to monitor my fatigue factor regularly. I've also learned that walking serves as an anti-depressant; therefore, the highest use of any day is a walk. Walking also serves as a de-stresser.

Stress Is a Pain in the Neck

To prevent disease it's important to keep track of acute stress, because some illnesses that begin as stress related can become organic. How you talk about things can provide clues to potential physical problems, too. For instance, Marya, whose husband left her for another woman, died six months later at the age of thirty-nine of a massive heart attack. She'd often said, "It just killed me. That man broke my heart."

If she could have handled her disillusionment, her betrayal, her stress, her loss, she may have been able to speak about what happened to her in ways that may have had a healing effect. If she could have released the corrosive anger and resentment she held against her husband, she may have paid better attention to what was happening with her heart in time to get medical help.

What are your favorite statements that refer to illness or parts of the body? Do you use metaphors like "She makes me sick," "I'm really fed up with that kid," "I get a kick out of him," "My ex is a real pain in the neck," "She'll talk your ear off if you let her," "My boss really grates on my nerves," "Patience my ass, I'm going to kill something!" Do you have a tennis elbow? What is your Achilles heel? Is your heart easily broken? Watch your words; casual statements can work in the subconscious to function as a kind of self-fulfilling prophecy.

An easy way to neutralize these negative statements is to add, "And I'm getting better at taking care of these stressful things." Any effective program of recovery includes stress management techniques such as regular exercise, relaxation techniques like autogenics or meditation, and cultivating a support group. If your current family isn't as supportive as you would like, consider creating an intentional family, where you seek out and choose the other people you need to fulfill your support needs. Fred found that his AA sponsor became a kind of surrogate father for him in his first year of recovery.

Massage is an increasingly important tool for stress management and for people in recovery. Not only does massage release tight muscles and assist the body to relax, but also it provides therapeutic touch in a safe and nonsexual context. Those in recovery who are not in intimate relationships find that a weekly massage prevents the buildup of touch-hunger and reduces vulnerability. People with eating disorders in particular, who are literally out-of-touch with their bodies, find that massage helps them understand, accept, and appreciate their physical selves. For those who are unfamiliar with or wary of legitimate therapeutic massage, foot reflexology and back-chair massage, which do not require undressing, provide a comfortable introduction to this powerful de-stresser.

Another physically relaxing experience is the isolation or float tank, which provides a distraction-free neutral environment. It offers deep relaxation to those who, because of a history of physical abuse, are uncomfortable with the idea of massage. There's also a wide variety of relaxation-oriented audio and video tapes as well as many biofeedback devices. For more information, see Michael Hutchison's books, *Mega-Brain* and *The Book of Floating*.

Stress can be avoided by understanding what your true priorities are and speaking up effectively for yourself. Novelist Herman Wouk warned, "Giving of yourself is happiness; squandering yourself is misery—the dividing line between the two is NO." Cultivate awareness about what you are feeling in response to stress and find appropriate ways to express it, rather than forcing yourself to be optimistic or cheerful. Resist pressure from others in your life to feel happy. Don't allow others to tell you to "cheer up," or to "have a good day," or otherwise to dictate how you should be feeling. Jane allowed her husband to invalidate her feelings with his comment, "If you think that's what you're feeling, you're kidding yourself."

Stress-Coping Strategies

It's important to develop your own stress-coping strategies. Here are some suggestions:

- Say no when asked to do something you don't want to do, and never take advice you don't agree with.
- Plan to do something each day that gives you energy, something you love to do, something creative just for you.
- Take deep slow breaths often, especially while on the phone,

in the car, or waiting. Use this time to relax and revitalize yourself.

- Learn to gracefully accept assistance from other people. Ask others for help. Delegate responsibility.
- Monitor your intake of sugar, salt, caffeine, and alcohol. Stop smoking.
- Take relaxation or meditation breaks. Take naps.
- Simplify your life; begin to eliminate the trivia. Include time for fun, spontaneity, and empty spaces. Set a realistic schedule allowing some transition time between activities.
- Practice the healing attitudes: acceptance, unconditional love, forgiveness, and laughter. Laugh more!

Stress diminishes when you begin to let go of the demands you place on yourself, your environment, and others to be different than they or you are at any moment. Demands are tremendous sources of stress. As you begin to release yourself from the conscious demands, other more subtle ways you pressure yourself will become more apparent.

As you regain control of your life in these small ways, you also learn to trust yourself. Trust in any relationship evolves from familiarity and repeated experiences, which provide a feeling of security and reliance that you will be treated well. Trusting yourself comes from learning to know yourself intimately and to understand that you can be relied on to protect and take good care of yourself. The next process can help you do just that.

Creative Process #18
Whom Can You Trust?

1. Take a large blank piece of drawing paper or newsprint and fold it in half so it opens like a book. On the right half of the inside page, using colored pens or crayons, sketch or draw a picture, diagram, or design of that part of your-

self that you can't trust. Work for five to ten minutes—
sketching without thinking or stopping.

2. Look at the picture or design and quickly add a title—the
first word or phrase that pops into your mind. Then, using
your journal or tape recorder, allow the picture or design
to tell you about itself, in its own words. Begin: "I am the
sketch of _____'s untrustworthiness." Continue
for five to ten minutes without thinking or stopping. Allow it to tell you the areas in your life that it affects. Allow
it to tell you what it seeks to do *for* you. Allow it to tell
you what it's most afraid of.

3. Ask it any questions you want. Record its answers immediately. Challenge or ask for clarification as you need to,
continuing the discussion as long as necessary.

4. Conclude this section by writing or saying your choice of
the following statements. "I am now willing (or not yet
willing) to acknowledge, accept, and embrace this part of
myself with all its fears—named and unnamed." Add any
other thoughts or feelings you have about this part of
yourself, including negative ones.

5. On the top fold of the paper, sketch or draw a picture,
diagram, or design of that part of yourself you can trust.
Continue for five to ten minutes—without thinking, without stopping.

6. Give the picture a title. Then allow it to tell you about
itself in its own words, and when and where it affects your
life. Some people think of the trustworthy part as their
inner wisdom. Begin: "I am the sketch of _____'s
trustworthy part." Write or talk steadily for five to ten
minutes. Think of yourself as taking dictation.

7. Ask it questions such as, How do I interfere with your
influence in my life? How can I learn to allow you to work
more freely in my life? Would you give me a specific physical signal when you're guiding me?

8. Write or say the following: "I am now willing (or not yet
willing) to acknowledge, accept, and embrace this trustworthy part of myself."

9. Record a discussion between the two parts of yourself and see what they have to say to each other.

10. Conclude this exercise by writing or saying, "I am now willing (or not yet willing) to acknowledge, accept, and embrace both these parts of myself."

The preceding process opens the way for an ongoing dialogue with your inner wisdom, which can lead to greater health and well-being.

Paying attention to the inner dimension of health and well-being reflected in your thoughts, feelings, and words does not replace conventional medical help. Have you determined if there is any physical condition affecting your recovery? New research, for instance, shows that many obsessive-compulsive and manic-depressive disorders may have a hereditary or biochemical component that can be controlled by medication. Many eating disorders may be allergy or food-sensitivity related. If you need medical treatment or surgery, get a second or third opinion. If surgery or other medical treatment is the most advisable thing to do, cooperate as Katy did.

Whether or not your recovery requires medical help, you will always benefit from seeking more information about your health issues and by fully participating in all aspects of your own well-being.

Food for Thought

Again, these questions are just to consider, not to ponder.

- Do you take good care of your physical body?
- Are you willing to look inward?
- Are you willing to get to know yourself?
- Are you ready to utilize your illnesses for growth?
- Are you willing to monitor your stress?
- Do you handle your stress constructively?
- Are you ready to learn to trust yourself?
- Are you fully participating in your recovery?

·10·

What You See Is
What You Get

The imagination has been called "The Scissors of the Mind," and it is ever cutting, cutting, cutting, day by day, the pictures man sees there, and sooner or later he meets his own creations in his outer world. Whatever man feels deeply or images clearly, is impressed upon the subconscious mind, and carried out in minutest detail.

FLORENCE SCOVEL SHINN

WYSIWYG is a strange new word spawned by the computer field. It means *what you see* on your computer screen *is what you get* when you print out the page. WYSIWYG is also true for human beings; what we visualize or can see happening in our mind's eye is much more likely to come true than something we can't envision. To achieve our desires and goals we need to feel and see them clearly.

Another word from the world of computers also applies to the reality of what we create in our lives. GIGO means garbage in; garbage out. If you feed your mind with self-generated scenes and visions representing illness, addiction, relapse, and the worst possible outcome, then those things are more likely to occur. My mother often told me, "What you think and feel, you bring into form. Where your thought is, there you are, for you are your consciousness, and what you meditate upon, you become."

The recovery programs that use aversion therapy or scare tactics may achieve temporary results; ultimately, however, the individual needs to switch to a positive focus to ensure quality of life. Anticipating disaster may soften possible disappointment from events that may turn out badly, but "disaster thinking" also may help to bring about unhappy consequences.

Positive thinking, a positive mental attitude, and affirmations are prescribed as antidotes, or as panaceas, for negativity. These prescriptions, however, are often misused or misunderstood. Sometimes positive thinking or having a positive mental attitude is used as a way of avoiding one's true feelings or as a sophisticated form of denial.

Affirming the Positive

The positive statements known as affirmations are powerful, but can become a what-you-*say*-is-what-you-get form of wish-fulfillment. Sometimes affirmations are used as a way of manipulating yourself or the universe to try to get your own way or just to accumulate material gain. Those who claim to hate affirmations are usually those who tried them and didn't get the results they thought they wanted.

Unfortunately, much popular teaching about affirmations leads to misinterpretation or oversimplification. Abusing the principles of affirmations results in unhappiness. "I now weigh one hundred pounds," is an example of an irresponsible affirmation. Judith's friend who used this affirmation daily became ill and did indeed end up weighing one hundred pounds, but the price she paid was a loss of good health and a diminished quality of life. One young man who desired $23,000 received exactly this amount as compensation for his injuries in a traffic accident.

When thinking about a specific desire, ask yourself, "What is the quality of experience I am seeking?" If I desire to look and feel slim and attractive, then that needs to be the focus of the affirmation, not an arbitrary number on the scale. If I want more money, I need to focus on what I'd spend the money for. Better yet is asking the next question: "What is the experience I am seeking through looking and feeling slim and attractive (or through having more money)?"

Affirmations do work. They are among the most powerful mental tools you can employ. But it's important to use them responsibly. Affirmations are not just positive statements. Every time you open your mouth to speak, you are affirming something. Remember that the next time you hear someone say "I'm such a klutz" or "I'm the kind of a person who gets results" or "My name is Jean. I am a compulsive overeater." Those statements perpetuate and affirm a negative state of being. A better affirmation for me may be, "I am a recovering compulsive overeater." After two to three years in therapy or a support group the best affirmation will simply be, "I am Jean."

People not only reflect their beliefs through the words they say, but also they end up making laws for themselves. Aaron, for example, repeatedly affirmed, "I never can find a parking place when I really need one." That's the law in his universe. Elaina, on the other hand, often said, "I usually find good parking." That idea became the law in her universe. As she's looking for that parking place she visualizes someone pulling out just as she arrives to slip into that spot. She used to visualize an empty parking place, but often saw someone else park there just before she could. Aaron believes Elaina is just lucky.

Every time you open your mouth to speak
you are affirming something.

The best context for the conscious use of affirmations is not in finding parking, but in seeking spiritual development, in clearing yourself as a channel for greater good for yourself, and in the service of others. There's much similarity between prayer and affirmation; they both consist of a request to God or to the universe.

The next Creative Process can help you build responsible affirmations.

Creative Process #19
Affirmation-Building

1. Begin by thinking about what you really want. Make a list of all your desires, from the specific to the general: "I want a new computer. I wish somebody would give me some lilacs. I'd like to quit smoking. I'd love to have a new red Camaro. I'd like to be more patient. I want good health. I'd like someone to love me. I want to be happy." Play with these wishes and dreams for five to ten minutes. Try not to censor or control the process. The list does not have to be definitive. Look back at some of the earlier processes you did to stimulate ideas.

2. Pick one want or desire to use as the basis for creating an affirmation. Make sure you're really open to receiving what you say you want. Ask yourself, "Am I willing to have that happen in my life?" Some of the specific things on the list may be things you can easily get for yourself, such as lilacs. Other more general ones may need further clarification before a good affirmation can be created. Happiness, for instance. How will you know when that comes true for you? How can you measure happiness? Knowing what you really want, and *how you will know when you get it*, often is the most difficult part of this process.

3. Build your affirmation in the present tense, using words that feel right for you. Avoid using a negative construction. The subconscious does not hear negative words, so "I am not addicted to cigarettes" is internalized by the subconscious as "I am addicted to cigarettes."

   Another kind of negative construction entails trying to get rid of something. "I am now free of the desire to smoke" sounds positive, but results in a vacuum; becoming free of something leaves an empty space. Nature, they say, abhors a vacuum, so a better affirmation would incorporate something more positive: "Now that I'm becoming free from the desire to smoke, I enjoy deep breathing, clean-smelling clothes, and fresh breath."

4. Incorporate an attitude of gratitude into your affirmation: "I now give thanks for my increasing freedom from the desire to smoke and for my enjoyment of breathing deeply, wearing clean-smelling clothes, and having fresh breath." Add other phrases that serve as affirmation enhancers, such as ". . . on a daily basis," ". . . whether I see it or not," and ". . . in accordance with the divine plan."

5. Increase the power of your affirmation by repeating it to yourself as you walk, or run, or dance. Visualize your desire as a regular part of your life; let yourself feel the joy and satisfaction of that good thing happening.

Powerful Affirmations

Here are some sample affirmations you can use as ideas:

- I am only addicted to loving myself; nothing has power over me. I am secure and free.
- I relax and allow life to flow. I am enthusiastic about life and filled with energy.
- In my world all is well. Whatever I need will always be here. I accept my good without guilt.
- I am always under direct inspiration. I now make wise choices and right decisions quickly.
- I now take loving care of the hungry child within me and make peace among my many other selves.
- I am worthy of experiencing love and fulfillment in all areas of my life. I love, trust, and accept myself.
- My cup runneth over with love and fulfillment.
- I increasingly find it easier to relax deeply. I wake up each morning feeling refreshed and energized.
- I now surrender the burden of carrying the emotional weight of other people.

My favorite affirmation is, "All things I seek are now seeking me." It's general enough that it saves me from impatience, of wondering when it's going to happen. I've discovered that it's best not to try to control the time factor, but to make my affirmation, then let go of the results. Things seem to happen more easily, more gracefully when I'm smart enough to remove my resistance and my expectations by not dictating how and when a wish or goal or desire should happen.

Sarah's best affirmation is, "I now give thanks for an increasing abundance of love, joy, and fulfillment in all my relationships." Geraldine affirmed for "Prosperity, financial abundance, cash, checks, and currency." Judith wanted "Expanded creativity, plus interesting and rewarding new freelance jobs and opportunities." Hannah asked for "Good health and good health habits in my body and in my life."

Fred wasn't sure he believed in affirmations, but decided it might be fun to test it out by trying to get the red Camaro he'd always wanted. So, every day for several months, Fred wrote, "I am now having fun with my new red Camaro." Fred told some of his friends about playing around with affirmations to get a red Camaro, knowing that he affirmed it every time he talked about it. He looked for a picture to help him visualize having it; he even went to a toy store and found a plastic model of a Camaro. He enjoyed assembling it and painting it cherry red; it sat on the workbench in his shop as a visual reminder of what he wanted.

Eventually Fred became busy with other projects; he stopped repeating the affirmation; the plastic model drifted out of sight under a pile of wood shavings. One day in a frenzy of spring cleaning, Fred swept off his workbench and spotted the little red toy car. As he picked it up, he laughed out loud in recognition that he had indeed created exactly the new red Camaro he had affirmed for.

The day his affirmation came true was the day he had walked into the toy store and bought it for himself. Both the words he'd used and his attitude toward having it had emphasized fun and playing around. Never had he visualized himself actually driving it or putting gas in it.

Fred discovered that the universe in which affirmations work is full of cosmic humor and, like the world of computers, a strange kind of literal-mindedness. Fred also appreciated that the ability to create his true vision of a red Camaro was more important than actually driving one.

Vision Plus Action Equals Results

Vision must be coupled with action to get results, and creating responsible affirmations is one level of taking action. It requires us to define our dreams and to risk reaching for them. It's important, however, to keep that dream or goal alive by taking other small actions.

One of my long-term dreams, for instance, has been to travel. My hope chest, as a teenager, consisted of a battered cardboard carton full of travel folders. Mexico's Mayan ruins particularly intrigued me, and Angel Falls in Venezuela, and Machu Picchu in Peru. My dream of world travel was sidetracked by an early marriage and raising children, although I often daydreamed of traveling in Mexico.

Then I began a long journey, that of addiction, self-discovery, and recovery, followed by divorce. I dreamed, affirmed, and worked to develop a freelance business doing what I loved doing: writing and teaching. My dreams of travel and of Mexico faded for a while.

That's what happens to dreams without action. The action part, however, doesn't have to be a giant step or even a deliberate one. My forgotten dream of Mexico got an unexpected boost when I received framed photographs of the Mayan pyramid and El Caracol, the observatory, at Chichen Itza. Every day, whether I consciously saw them or not, I had that vision before me on the bookcase in my office.

When a friend began leading small groups to the Yucatan, the northeastern tip of Mexico, I longed to go, but felt I couldn't afford it. However, I'm also aware that whenever I'm using the excuse of lack of time or lack of money not to do something, it's never the real reason. Therefore, I said "Count me in."

I began reading John Steven's *Incidents of Travel in the Yucatan* every night before sleeping, and I took one more small action: I purchased my first passport. Even though a passport is not a necessity for travel to Mexico, it was an important step toward actualizing my dream of world travel.

My passport traveled in my moneybelt on the flight to Mexico and on my excursion to Chichen Itza and six other Mayan archaeological sites. My hope-chest dream had come true. Now that that dream materialized, I'm working on a vision of Machu Picchu and Angel Falls, taking action by posting maps of Peru and Venezuela on my office wall. And as long as I'm dreaming, my vision is expanding to include a healthy relationship with an interesting man; I'd like to find a journey-oriented travel partner with an itchy foot and a spirit of adventure.

Creating Relationships

Creating healthy relationships is another area of challenge, nowadays, especially for those in recovery from addiction. Many existing models for relationships don't really work very well anymore; nobody knows what to expect, what role to play, or how to play it.

Old relationship models include the playgirl or boy-toy relationship when one person is seen as an object or trophy—and the more traditional man-as-breadwinner/woman-as-housewife relationship. These models have become increasingly unsatisfying and obsolete. One of the problems in these kinds of relationships is that even though the obsessive focus of the couple's energy seems to be on taking care of each other, that focus and energy is essentially selfish.

Healthy relationships consist of two people who identify

and solve their own problems with the loving support of the other, and where the partners do not try to save the other from the pain of their difficulties and learning experiences, but offer help to each other in their struggles through the pain. "It is a fact," said Irene Claremont de Castillejo, "that in any partnership, if one of the partners becomes quite clear . . . what it is that the situation requires, the chances are it will not even be necessary to voice it; the other will somehow . . . comply, with no words said."

Although it is true that in relationships we train people how to treat us, it's also true that people treat us as they have been treated or would like to be treated. Therefore, it's useful for those seeking a partner to have healed much of their relationship to their past.

Jane's first healing affirmation was, "I am now willing to stop dating men who don't respect women." Then Jane went through a phase when it seemed as if all she could do was say no to any relationship. This was the opposite of her usual behavior, but it did not feel much like progress because she often felt lonely. She understood intellectually that for people who can't say no, their yes has no validity, but that didn't help much.

One day Jane started to feel more positive when it occurred to her that for the first time in her life she was able to reject unhealthy relationships and was willing to wait until one really felt right. Her next affirmation became a joyful, "Yes! I can say no."

If you're looking for a good relationship, you need to watch how you talk about your desires. Fred often said, "It would take a mighty peculiar woman to love me." Then he couldn't understand why he attracted a variety of mighty peculiar women.

Because many traditional models for relationships no longer are functional or desirable nowadays, people must be willing to create new models. The creative mode, you may remember, is characterized by a lack of limits; it can be fun, but it is also chaotic, scary, and risky. Relationships in general are considered risky; relationships when you are creating or co-creating them as you go are exciting, but present an even greater risk.

It is important to have healed previous relationships before you embark on another. Katy discovered a useful principle that applies to both jobs and relationships. "The way I used to do it created disconcerting results," she said. "I'd quit one job before looking for another one, but I'd try to line up a new relationship before ending my current one." Now she puts it like this, "Regarding jobs: I *do not* end one before looking for another. Regarding relationships: it's important to me to complete or end one relationship before beginning another." A person's job, by the way, is a relationship with work. The best job is one that combines creative interest with one's work.

Self-knowledge and profound self-acceptance will help you to attract and nurture good relationships with others. Most of the Creative Processes in this book are designed to help you create good relationships with your work, your job, or other creative endeavors. If you feel reasonably comfortable with your relationship with yourself, the following process is one you can use to go after the job, or the relationship, you desire.

Creative Process #20
Creating What You Want

1. Take two sheets of paper. On the first sheet, put your name. On the second sheet, put the name of the kind of relationship or job you're looking for. As fast as possible, cover the first page with a list of words that relate to who you are and the second page with a list of words that express what you're looking for. Spend a few minutes on each page.

2. From those idea sheets, create a wish list for the relationship or job you're seeking. When that list satisfies you, take each item on that list and write a positive statement, if you can, about your willingness to *have* that in a relationship or job, and another sentence about your willingness to *give* that in a relationship or job.

3. Do a revised list of what you want; create a relationship or job description in the style of a classified ad. Then draw a circle around it, date it, and sign it. Put it in your desk calendar to look at six months from now, or write yourself a note reminding yourself to review it again in six months.
4. If you are currently in an unsatisfying job or relationship, consider these questions: What is the quality of experience you're seeking? Are you willing to experience the satisfaction you seek in your present job or relationship?

Affirming Your Life

One woman in my Writing for Recovery workshop complained bitterly that her ambition to become a minister was thwarted by her poverty and the prejudice of those in the hierarchy of her church against female clergy. She lacked the money to enroll in divinity school, and the administration seemed to discourage women from applying anyway.

I challenged the assumption that she needed anyone's stamp of approval to minister to others. If she sincerely wanted to help others, to minister to them, she could do that no matter where she was and no matter what she did. I'm not implying that poverty should be celebrated or prejudice tolerated. However, her ambition appeared to be to become a minister rather than a wish to minister to others.

Cheri, on the other hand, is a waitress who provides comfort and compassion to her customers; she serves bread and wine as a sacrament, not in an obvious or dramatic way, but in her heart and in her attitude of service. She begins each day with a simple prayer, "Bless all those whose lives touch mine." A minister is one who ministers to others, not a person with a pulpit. Cheri ministers to her customers every day.

Albert Schweitzer said, "The only ones among you who will be really happy are those who will have sought and found how to serve." That idea points up a vital aspect of the fully functioning personality—that sense of finding a higher purpose for one's life.

Teaching in a formal or informal way, such as volunteering a few hours a week to a literacy program as Hannah does, answering the phones at a crisis center or community referral service as Judith did, or tutoring disadvantaged children for your school district, could serve that purpose, but only if it reflects your genuine interest. If your community service fits you and serves your needs, others are more likely to experience being helped.

Bruce is active in several environmental awareness organizations; he recycles newspaper and aluminum cans and avoids buying overpackaged food items. Jane works eight days a month at a home for homeless women and children. Elaina volunteers at the infant nursery of her local hospital; she spends four hours a week holding, rocking, and loving babies who have AIDS or other terminal illnesses. Fred is a Big Brother for a twelve year old from an alcoholic family. Aaron loans his rocking animals to the children's room of his neighborhood library; "My animals need the exercise," Aaron says. Elaina, Fred, and Aaron all feel that these acts enrich their lives.

Even Schweitzer did not think of his service in Africa as altruistic, but more as his way of affirming his own life. "Affirmation of life is the spiritual act by which man ceases to live unreflectively and begins to devote himself to his life with reverence in order to raise it to its true value. To affirm life is to deepen, to make more inward, and to exalt the will to live."

Pure altruism probably does not exist. Those like Schweitzer or Mother Teresa who have dedicated their lives to the service of others—some may say they have sacrificed their lives for those others—reflect a true value of their lives. I doubt they would agree with the idea of sacrificing themselves; their lives are chosen and are fulfilling for them. Whatever you do in service of that higher purpose must not feel like a sacrifice. It must be an honest expression of your values.

Living your life in service of your higher good, and thereby setting an example to others of a life well lived, may be enough. That sense of a higher purpose in what you do is the important ingredient. If you have that, you don't need to worry about its value to others. Value to others is not the issue. Finding that higher purpose and actualizing your dreams is what really counts.

The following Creative Process can help you sort out relationship and job choices or work through problems and difficulties. It can also provide an opportunity to try on a few dreams for size.

Creative Process #21
Future Fantasy

1. Pick a time one or two years in the future. Begin by writing or saying, "The date is _____. I am ____years old." Describe your ideal life of the future including work and relationships. Write or speak in the present tense, as if it were happening right now. Have fun with it; after all, this is a fantasy. Don't be bound by facts or too much so-called reality. Then keep writing or talking, without thinking and without stopping, for five to ten minutes.

2. Maintain your present-tense focus on that time in the future as you briefly reflect on something you wanted more of in your life one to two years ago. Then write or talk about how it feels now to have more of that in your life. Don't write about how you got more, but just about how it feels to have more. Aim for a stream-of-consciousness flow as you write or speak.

3. Again reflect on something you experienced as a problem or difficulty one to two years ago. Then write or talk about how it feels no longer to experience it as a problem or difficulty, not how you solved or overcame it.

4. Look around at the significant people in your now-future life—make them up if you want to. Write or talk about how

they feel about your ability to create more of what you want and your being able to solve your problems and difficulties.

5. Complete this sentence without thinking and without stopping: "One of the most important things I've learned in the last year or two is _____."

There's a follow-up question regarding whatever you're seeking more of: How are you taking care of that which you already have?

This Creative Process can function as an aid to visualizing, as a self-fulfilling prophecy, and as a way to help make career or even relationship decisions. For decision making, when there's two alternatives and no clear choice, pick one to do a future fantasy with. What you're looking for as you do this process is that half-line of information that illuminates the issue, the "Aha, so that's what's going on" response, which can help you make today's decision.

Food for Thought

More questions to consider and contemplate:

- What is the quality of experience you're seeking?
- What thoughts and feelings are you bringing into form?
- Where is your thought now?
- What do you choose to meditate upon?
- What do you choose to think and feel?
- What is your imagination picturing?
- What are you feeling deeply?
- What are you picturing clearly?

· 11 ·

Choosing Freedom
and Joy

*A woman, in her sleep, dreamt Life stood before her,
and held in each hand a gift—in the one Love, in the
other Freedom. And she said to the woman, "Choose!"
And the woman waited long; and she said, "Freedom!"
And Life said, "Thou has well chosen. If thou hadst
said, 'Love' I would have given thee that thou didst ask
for; and I would have returned to thee no more. Now
the day will come when I shall return. In that day I
shall bear both gifts in one hand." The woman, in her
sleep, laughed.* OLIVE SCHREINER

C HOICE IS the hallmark of the place we finally come to,
the place that's worth struggling to achieve. Today it
could be said that Life offers us a choice between Recovery and Freedom.

Recovery embraces all the many aspects of the temporary
change called self-improvement. Freedom embraces profound
self-acceptance, personal power, creative expression, joy, and
well-being.

Some people will settle for recovery alone. It is their choice.
Others will choose the uncertain path of freedom.

On the path of freedom, the uncovering and expressing of

your true character is an on-going challenge that requires daily attention, but not daily obsession. The process of discovering your true character moves you from denial through pain, chaos, and upheaval to a graceful, unconscious way of living—where all you've learned is easily reflected in how you act on a daily basis, and where you acknowledge and take care of your feelings when they occur, or at least when they surface.

Choosing freedom does not mean that life lacks problems, pain, and sorrow; it just means that everyday problems are readily faced and dealt with; eventually you learn to accept and feel hurt without resentment, and to weep without getting stuck in self-pity. Any former identification of yourself as an alcoholic, addict, or overeater, for example, has evolved into thinking of yourself as a human being whose history may include certain compulsive behavior, addictive involvement, or other difficulties. Your well-being or recovery, however, has become integrated into the living of a full and productive life.

I'm not suggesting becoming complacent about any positive changes that have been achieved, nor do I have any quarrel with the Twelve Steps or any other program. I am suggesting giving up the idea of perfection as a goal and recognizing when your improvement or recovery is good enough and it's time to move on. It is important to know yourself so well that whatever needs to be done on a regular basis to ensure continued well-being is done without struggle.

Will you choose freedom?

Like a diabetic who must live within the restrictions of diet and medication, the person who seeks to trade the pursuit of self-improvement for the challenge of freedom doesn't waste energy fighting any restrictions imposed by a recovery program. The alcoholic abstains from alcohol; the compulsive overeater may avoid certain foods; those with a history of being abused do not allow others to mistreat them.

These acts are done not only to survive but also to protect the quality of life. There's a subtle shift from the struggle to get through each day to an easy acceptance of whatever each day brings, an awareness of daily well-being, and an understanding of personal choices and priorities. Such an understanding was expressed by Robert Fulghum, a retired Unitarian minister:

> My lot concerns the dying and the dead. The hospital room, the mortuary, the funeral service, the cemetery. . . . What I know of such things explains why I don't waste much life time mowing grass or washing cars or raking leaves or making beds or shining shoes or washing dishes. It explains why I don't honk at people who are slow to move at green lights. And why I don't kill spiders. There isn't time or need for all this.

Designing Your Life

"The secret of a full life," according to diarist Anais Nin, "is to live and relate to others as if they might not be there tomorrow. It eliminates the vice of procrastination, the sin of postponement, failed communication."

Ultimately, you know not only what you have the time and need for, but what a full life means to you. You have enough self-knowledge to know what you need to do to live sanely, which may or may not include ongoing therapy. Geraldine, for example, still attends Gamblers Anonymous on a twice-weekly basis. Jane, who is finally emerging from a long, voluntary abstinence from serious relationships, is beginning to socialize more and goes to group therapy only once a month. Fred continues to go to his AA meeting every week.

Debbie, however, like many new young alcoholics, experienced what's being called spontaneous recovery. Although she has three years of enthusiastic sobriety behind her, she never became involved with a group. She does, however, work a good daily program that functions without formal support. Her self-directed program includes all the principles of recovery, such as making amends, having support people, taking inventory, and sharing her experience, strength, and hope with other young drug addicts and alcoholics. The only low point for Debbie has been with some militant friends who, threatened by her independence, still predict relapse for her unless she attends AA.

Aaron, also independent, continues to educate himself. Increasingly he's able and willing to speak for himself and allow himself to know what he wants. He no longer automatically volunteers to feel bad when things do not happen to suit him. Although he enjoys himself more frequently and no longer takes everything that happens personally, self-pity is still a trap for him. Nevertheless, Aaron, who formerly resisted change and assumed that any change would be negative, experienced a breakthrough when he began to allow for the possibility that things may change for the better.

Those, like Fred, who have struggled for awareness and self-knowledge, have found that it's possible to live in the active mode, so that the boredom and passivity that led to secondary feelings of anxiety, resentment, self-pity, and nostalgia are seldom experienced. When those energy-robbing thoughts and feelings do threaten him, he recognizes the old patterns and readily takes the necessary steps to regain his freedom.

Upgrading Your Problems

Hannah's most recent problem, for instance, was her increasing anger and frustration about the yuppie-wannabe materialism of her grown children—especially at Christmas time. She decided to try the geographical cure and escaped to a remote island retreat for the last two weeks of December. The first year she felt as if she were fleeing for her life; by the third year, however, the healing solitude she experienced on the island had changed her point of view.

No longer did the holiday madness starting in October annoy her; no longer did she resent her children's values; no longer did she feel like running away. What she did experience was a sense of moving happily toward her year-end retreat and a renewed appreciation of her family just as they were. When Hannah traded the problems of duty and resentment for the challenge of voluntary simplicity, her attitude toward the differences between her family and herself became more compassionate.

When the vain pursuit of improvement is relinquished, compassion and detachment become the norm. One seeks neither to rescue others nor to be saved from oneself. The individual is able and willing to ask for help or to extend a helping hand when appropriate, and does not take offense or feel rejected when a request for help or offer of assistance gets a negative response. According to Abraham Maslow, "The fully functioning personality can be, when the objective situation calls for it, comfortably disorderly, anarchic, vague, doubtful, uncertain, indefinite, approximate, inexact or inaccurate." The fully functioning personality lives in a world of choices. The individual may not be totally free of old patterns, but does experience being able to choose to spend his or her energy in creative ways rather than in compulsive ones.

A mature, whole person evolves from painful self-awareness through self-consciousness to self-analysis and ultimately to what Maslow called "unself-conscious expression." The necessity to define problems, to name or label them, diminishes. The feelings of pushing, shoving, and striving, and the disciplining, calculating, manipulating of oneself or others drops away. The struggle is over.

The individual is content to live peacefully in the here and now, knowing, as the Buddhist saying goes, that "the light you seek is in your own lantern." One neither runs away from, nor denies, one's own reality, but, like Hannah, seeks to move forward and take action toward something better—without any attachment to having those actions happen in a set time or in a set manner, but with an openness to other un-thought-of possibilities. True change results in the development of peace of mind, a sense of humor, tolerance for others, a willingness to embrace adversity, and a capacity to do what needs to be done next.

Taking the Next Step

On that initial trip to Mexico I climbed the steep Temple of the Magician pyramid at Uxmal two days in a row. The previous day my companions had said, "You've gotta be kidding" to attempt such a thing, but I'd managed to do it and felt determined to stand on top again. As I slowly hoisted myself up the high and narrow steps, with the hot sun increasing the difficulty of the task, I looked neither up nor down. I did have a vision of reaching the top, and I did stay in action, one step at a time.

As I reached the rough stone ledge surrounding the top platform, I moved to the shady side to enjoy viewing the ruins and jungle. A man half my age waited there. "I wanted to thank you," he said. "When I saw you up here yesterday, I'd given up the idea of climbing up here; it looked much too hard. But I figured if you could do it, anybody could." He grinned. "Now, how do I get down?" I told him first to watch how others did it, then to pick a style that looked compatible, and, most important, to look only at the next step down. Then take that one step.

Later, as I carefully picked my way down, following my advice, I enjoyed his back-handed compliment. An elderly Mexican couple watched my slow progress, then smiled and applauded as I neared the ground. I bowed and smiled back.

It had briefly occurred to me that I may be too old, too heavy, or too out of condition to attempt the steep climb in the jungle heat and humidity, but I knew I really wanted to do it. I'd been unwilling to let others' opinions deter me from my goal; I'd been totally willing not only to make a fool of myself but also to enjoy whatever happened—all significant principles in making dreams come true.

The following Creative Process can help to determine what your next step may be.

Creative Process #22
What's Happening in My Life?

1. Pick one general topic such as health, money, love, or career; or choose one specific focus such as your fitness program, your credit card debt, your primary relationship, or your job. Ask yourself:
   - Regarding _____, what do I want?
   - Regarding _____, what am I experiencing?
   - Regarding _____, what is interfering with my getting what I say I want?

   For each area of focus, repeat this series of questions at least three times. Automatically record your answers in a stream-of-consciousness manner. Keep the pencil moving on the paper the whole time, or keep the verbalization into the tape recorder going without holding back or censoring.

2. If you find that what you're experiencing evokes negative words such as "dissatisfaction," "rejection," or "hostility," then the challenge is to look at where in your life you may be withholding, or not being accepting, or not being calm and loving to others. Accept responsibility for creating what you are experiencing.

   Or, use the projection stream-of-consciousness process to find out more about what significance that word has in your life. "I am _____'s loneliness, (or fear, or dissatisfaction, or rejection)." Ask what its purpose is or what message it may have for you.

3. After you've processed the negatives, look for that half-line of information or insight that will lead toward the next step or some useful action. Or, ask yourself, What is my next step toward actualizing this dream?

   When you discover that next step, the next question is,

Am I willing to do that? If you're not willing, then it's time to let go of it for now and to do something else without penalizing yourself.

Actualizing Attitudes

In the actualizing mode you have an attitude of commitment toward your own well-being, but not with white-knuckled grimness. You experience no issues of control with yourself or others, just a willingness to try things, to make mistakes, to be wrong or fail—even to refuse to take that next step. No father-knows-best, or superwoman, or macho facades mask the full range of human feelings, behavior, and possibilities.

As Judith finally realized, the biggest trap for her was perfectionism. Therefore, she understood that she would probably never feel fully improved or recovered. She now profoundly accepts the fact that like everyone else she's a fallible, and possibly neurotic, human being. And, despite all that, she's usually willing to live a full and happy life.

Judith recognized that it was a waste of time for her to be preoccupied with recovery issues; she learned just to take care of each day as it occurred. She also understood that in her lifetime she would lead many lives, and all she needed to know was, What will I choose to do with my life today? Her other daily questions included, What do I need to do to take care of myself today? and What other things do I want or need to do? Judith, who used to be obsessed with regrets about yesterday or plans for tomorrow, now knows that today is the *only* day of the rest of her life.

Barometers of Well-Being

As people learn about what their well-being requires, they begin to understand the elements that function as barometers or signs of trouble. Judith found that her desire to tell people how heavy she used to be reflected her fear that people would expect too much of her if they assumed that she was normal. When she no longer needed to be perceived as special or different, she stopped showing her fat picture to others.

Some of my own well-being barometers include journal writing and taking myself outdoors for a walk. When I neglect to write in my journal, or when I find myself "too busy" to take a long walk at least four days a week, or when my food behavior gets weird, or when my need for solitude drifts into avoiding friends and family, or when my fingernails disappear overnight and I don't remember biting them off, then I need to stop and look at what's really going on with me. And I can often gauge my peace of mind by how I feel about delays while driving in traffic.

Another symptom of trouble for me is when I find myself wishing I were somewhere else; when I'm with people, I'd rather be alone; when I'm alone, I long for company. This increasing misalignment between where I am and where I wish I were reflects that I'm out of sync and need to become centered. Sometimes returning to my therapist for a while can reinforce my paying better attention to my well-being basics.

Life is uncertain; therefore, living with uncertainty is part of living in the so-called real world. Eventually you learn to accept whatever is happening around you and, more importantly, whatever is happening with you and within you. You don't have to like what's happening either in your world or in yourself, but you do have to acknowledge and validate all of it as you go along. In essence, you must accept and say yes to everything you find. To the extent that you are willing to do that is the extent to which you have a chance of staying relatively healthy in your relationship with yourself and the world.

Cultivating an open mind allows for the widest range of choices and options. Having an open mind doesn't mean abandoning responsibility. It does mean giving up perfectionism, rigidity, and the false idea that anything is all black or all white. It also means embracing uncertainty; I must let go of the idea that I'll ever know anything for sure. I am reasonably certain, however, that I'm never going to live long enough to do everything the hard way.

My goal is to experience feeling whole, not by masking or denying pain, but by expressing that pain in creative and transformative ways. Transmuting that pain through service to others, through artistic expression, or through other constructive action is essential because it provides a sense of higher purpose. Whenever I write a story or article, or stop what I'm doing to respond to a phone call from a student, whenever I volunteer my time to a regional arts organization, I remove myself from the center of the universe. Anytime I surrender to the creative moment my ego disappears and I experience true satisfaction and joy.

Joy Rising

Joy is not a fixed state. It is not a constant. It is not predictable. It can't be willed or manipulated into being. When I'm waiting for joy, it seldom occurs. Joy, however, can be courted. Keeping active and healthy, being creatively involved with satisfying work, and maintaining good relationships all increase the likelihood of encountering joy, of being swept away by bliss.

Serendipity, delight, pleasure, happiness, bliss, and joy all tend to happen more often, to sneak up on me, to surprise me, when I'm in the creative mode. There's a feeling I experience from time to time that I think of as joy rising. Like the effervescence in a glass of sparkling water, it begins to bubble up from somewhere within me. Often it begins with a tiny serendipitous moment, like when I find a penny on the sidewalk, or glimpse a rainbow, or hear the wholehearted, full-bellied laughter of my young grandsons.

My ability to enjoy those moments comes from some important things I've learned about myself. This self-knowledge takes the pressure off my relationships and keeps my expectations of myself and others reasonable. Maintaining balance in my relationships, and balance between work and play, seems to be my current challenge. In both work and play I aim for that delicate equilibrium between the boredom of not enough stimulation and the pressure of being overwhelmed. I try to keep my involvement with work playful; if an opportunity doesn't look like fun, I won't do it anymore.

Despite this genuine progress and these stated good intentions, I still tend to cope with boredom, pressure, and pain by using food as a mood changer. As the old French proverb observed, "The more things change, the more they remain the same." Despite all the ups and downs of dieting versus not dieting, I've come to accept that my weight may always be a variable. The biggest change for me is in how I feel about that reality. I never use it to keep me from doing what I want or need to do or as a stick to beat myself with.

This exemplifies the primary true change I have accomplished in the last fifteen years: a shift from operating primarily in the negative mode to operating primarily in the positive mode. However, I have finally given up the false and unrealistic Pollyanna pretense of one hundred percent positivity. I've found that it's usually enough to be feeling fifty-one percent positive.

When at times I feel fifty-one percent negative, I know that all I have to do to change how I'm feeling is make a tiny two-percent shift. That crucial two-percent shift up or down makes all the difference in my quality of life and my perception of myself and my world. That two-percent shift, however, is not necessarily easy to accomplish, even with access to all the wonderful Creative Processes in this book. Having them is one thing, choosing to use them is another.

A sign hangs on my office wall that says Nothing Is Worth More Than This Day. That maxim reminds me that each day is a mixed bag of experiences and feelings, of good and not-so-good encounters and events—and each day is a smorgasbord of choices. No matter what the circumstances, I can always choose to live each day as a creative act and be willing to be surprised by joy.

Creative Process #23
Plan for Today

Remember Creative Process #3 from chapter three, the four-part antidote to inertia? If you've worked through some of the Creative Processes, you have begun to know what kinds of things you need to be doing on a daily basis. Create your personalized version of the following suggestions. The goal is still to spend a minimum of two hours each day in any of these four ways.

1. Brisk walking, dancing, gardening, or other physical activity
2. Communicating thoughts and feelings
3. People contacts: in-person or telephone
4. Involvement in any creative endeavor: drawing, painting, gardening, or photography; knitting, woodworking, pottery, or other craft; writing poems, stories, or songs; playing a musical instrument or singing

Some time each day should be spent in active enjoyment of the little pleasures, the "petite happinesses." Aim for the right balance between time spent with others and time spent alone. Remember that creative involvement includes anything when you feel pleasure or enjoyment and where you lose track of time.

The next diagram (from chapter two) should look familiar, also. Combine the above items on your daily list with the rest of your daily tasks and pursuits. Account for most of your waking hours—sixteen of the daily twenty-four. Fit the items from your list into the diagram to monitor your quality of life.

	WANTING TO	NOT WANTING TO
DOING	A	B
NOT DOING	D	C

Paying attention to what's happening on a daily basis is the best way to ensure your ongoing quality of life.

On Making a Difference

Now that you have a tool kit of Creative Processes, every day you get a brand new chance, a chance to get up, to make your own choices, to make a difference. The primary difference you can make is to attend to your quality of life, to pay attention, and to set a good example for the other people in your life by making authentic choices for yourself. Artist Tasha Tudor, who lives alone with her art, her garden, and her animals, said, "I have the privilege of being alive in this wonderful world."

So do you. When you enjoy your life and live well, others will benefit. Every day you have the opportunity to invent your life. You create your past in your thoughts, your future in today's acts that affect tomorrow, and your present minute by minute.

Every day that you live fully and truly you make a difference. Every day that you spend living rather than engaged in a relentless pursuit of self-improvement is a small victory. When you attend to your own business rather than to that of others you create harmony. When you are willing to say a whole-hearted yes to life, it makes a difference not only for you but also for your family, your friends, and society as a whole.

I don't know whether you'll choose Freedom and create ways to make it work for you. Or maybe you'll just look at life more positively from now on. What's most important is that you become more comfortable with joy and satisfaction. After all, that's what you want, isn't it?

Food for Thought

- As a fully functioning personality, are you comfortable with your imperfections?
- Are you able to be comfortably disorderly, anarchic, vague, doubtful, uncertain, indefinite, approximate, inexact, or inaccurate?
- Are you unconditionally accepting of yourself?
- Are you creating enough joy and laughter for yourself?
- What are you choosing today?
- Will you choose Freedom?

Chapter Notes

CHAPTER ONE
1. Milton Mayeroff, *On Caring* (New York: Harper & Row, 1971).
2. Codependency definition from the first National Conference on Codependency in Scottsdale, Arizona, September 1989.

CHAPTER TWO
1. Sheldon Kopp, *If You Meet the Buddha on the Road, Kill Him!* (Palo Alto, CA: Science & Behavior Books, Inc., 1972).
2. John Enright, Grid based on 1974 ARC Seminar notes.

CHAPTER THREE
1. Stymean Karlen, Source unattributable. Quoted in a letter from a friend.
2. Reinhold Niebuhr, "Modern Education and Human Values" lecture series (Pittsburgh: University of Pittsburgh Press, 1948).

CHAPTER FOUR
1. Janette Rainwater, Ph.D., *You're In Charge! A Guide to Becoming Your Own Therapist* (Los Angeles: Guild of Tutors Press, 1979).
2. Carl Jung, *Modern Man in Search of a Soul* (New York: Harcourt Brace Jovanovich, 1933).
3. Albert Schweitzer, *Out of My Life and Thought* (New York: Henry Holt, 1949).
4. Hermann Hesse, *Siddhartha* (New York: New Directions, 1951).
5. Janet Burr, *Awaken Your Intuition* (Edmonds, WA: Intuition Trainings, 1986).

CHAPTER FIVE

1. Somerset Maugham, "The Treasure," in *The Mixture As Before* (New York: Doubleday Doran, 1940).

2. Anais Nin, *The Diary of Anais Nin* vol. 4 1944–1947 (New York: Harcourt Brace Jovanovich, 1971).

3. Katherine Mansfield. Source unattributable. From a clipping a student brought to class.

CHAPTER SIX

1. Martha Graham, *Martha Graham*, ed. Merle Armitage (Brooklyn, NY: Dance Horizons, 1966).

2. Hal Stone and Sidra Winkelman, *Embracing Our Selves* (San Rafael, CA: New World Library, 1989).

3. John Enright, *Enlightening Gestalt* (Mill Valley, CA: Pro Telos, 1980).

4. Ruth Rendell, British novelist. Source unattributable. From a clipping a student brought to class.

CHAPTER SEVEN

1. Irene Claremont de Castillejo, *Knowing Woman—A Feminine Psychology* (New York: Harper & Row, 1974).

2. Sheldon Kopp, *The Hanged Man* (Palo Alto, CA: Science & Behavior Books, Inc., 1975).

3. Leonard Shaw, Seattle therapist. From his December 1989 newsletter.

4. James Hilton. Source unattributable. From a clipping a student brought to class.

5. Nin, *Diary of Anais Nin*.

CHAPTER EIGHT

1. Robert Francis, *Frost: A Time to Talk* (Amherst, MA: University of Massachusetts Press, 1972).

2. Michael Ryan, "A Hidden Talent," *Parade Magazine*, May 28, 1989.

3. Carl Rogers, *Carl Rogers on Encounter Groups* (New York: Harper & Row, 1970).

4. James L. Adams, *Conceptual Blockbusting* (New York: W.W. Norton, 1974) references the work of psychologist Frank Barron.

5. Adams, *Conceptual Blockbusting*.

6. Ted Kennedy, *Parade Magazine*, June 11, 1989.

7. Tony Curtis quote from a television interview.
8. Eric Hoffer, *Reflections on the Human Condition* (New York: Harper & Row, 1973).
9. Frederick Franck, *The Zen of Seeing—Seeing/Drawing as Meditation* (New York: Random House, 1973).
10. Phyllis Battelle, "Therapy Through Fiction." Hearst Special News Service feature.
11. 1985 Southern Methodist University study mentioned on a radio program.
12. The Center of Arts Therapy was featured on a television program.
13. "Creativity—The Pleasure Factor," *Vogue* Magazine, 1984, quote from Teresa Amabile, Ph.D.
14. Nin, *Diary of Anais Nin.*

CHAPTER NINE
1. Kenneth Pelletier, *Mind As Healer, Mind As Slayer* (New York: Dell Publishing, 1977).
2. Glenn Affleck, *Brain/Mind Bulletin*, October 1987.
3. Lydia Temoshek, *Redbook* Magazine, May 1988.
4. de Castillejo, *Knowing Woman.*
5. Maggie Lettvin, *Maggie's Back Book* (New York: Houghton Mifflin, 1976).
6. Michael Hutchison, *Megabrain: New Tools and Techniques for Brain Growth and Mind Expansion* (New York: Morrow, 1986), and *The Book of Floating: Exploring the Private Sea* (New York: Morrow, 1984).
7. Herman Wouk. Source unattributable. From a magazine clipping a student brought to class.

CHAPTER TEN
1. Florence Scovel Shinn, *The Game of Life and How to Play It* (New York: Gerald J. Rickard, 1941).
2. de Castillejo, *Knowing Woman.*
3. Schweitzer, *Out of My Life.*

CHAPTER ELEVEN
1. Olive Schreiner, *Dreams* (Little Leather Library, 1890).
2. Robert L. Fulghum, *All I Really Needed to Know I Learned in Kindergarten* (New York: Villard Books/Random House, 1986).

3. Nin, *Diary of Anais Nin*.

4. Abraham Maslow, *The Farther Reaches of Human Nature* (New York: The Viking Press, 1971).

5. Betty Rollin, with Tasha Tudor, From an NBC *Today* interview, August 2, 1990.

Recommended Reading

Awaken Your Intuition, Janet Burr (Edmonds, WA: Intuition Trainings, 1986). This is an easy-to-understand home study course complete with cassette tape.

The Creative Journal, Lucia Cappachione (Athens, OH: Swallow Press Books, 1979). The author is an art therapist. The book is full of inspiring journal exercises combining art and writing.

Knowing Woman—A Feminine Psychology, Irene Claremont de Castillejo (New York: Harper & Row, 1974). This is not easy to read but worth the struggle, especially for women.

The Zen of Seeing—Seeing /Drawing as Meditation, Frederick Franck (New York: Random House, 1973). A wonerful eye-opener about creative involvement in general and drawing the natural way in particular. It is not just for the artist.

The Path of Least Resistance—Learning to Become the Creative Force in Your Own Life, Robert Fritz (New York: Ballentine Books, 1989). Steps in the creative process.

If You Meet The Buddha on the Road, Kill Him!, Sheldon Kopp (Palo Alto, CA: Science & Behavior Books, 1972). This book is helpful for anyone dealing with pain either physical or emotional. Any book by Sheldon Kopp is interesting.

You're In Charge! A Guide to Becoming Your Own Therapist, Janette Rainwater, Ph.D. (Los Angeles: Guild of Tutors Press, 1979). Empowering exercises leading to true change.

The Game of Life and How to Play It, Florence Scovel Shinn (New York: Gerald J. Rickard, 1941). Old-fashioned, metaphysical, and Christian, but valuable for those interested in the power of affirmations.

Embracing Our Selves—The Voice Dialogue Manual, Hal Stone, Ph.D. & Sidra Winkelman, Ph.D. (San Rafael, CA: New World Library, 1989). Valuable processes to get better acquainted with the selves that live within you.

Acknowledgments

THIS BOOK owes its life to more than the ideas and vision of its author. First and foremost I'd like to express my grateful appreciation to all the students of my Magic Journal and Creative Recovery workshops and groups.

Special acknowledgments go to Deborah Nucci, who volunteered plentiful hugs, tough-love feedback, vital information, and other essentials. Thanks to John Enright for permission to adapt ARC Seminar exercises; to Carly Ayres for introducing me to the principles of affirmations; and to both Nan Netherland, M.S.W., and Sally Hartley, alcoholism counselor, for encouragement, feedback, and friendship.

Other therapists who have supported this effort include Christy Cave, M.S.W.; Kathryn Darner, M.S.W.; and Mary Baird Carlson, Ph.D.

Kathryn Nelson provided enthusiastic secretarial help. Ray Higgs contributed friendship plus an introduction to Julia Newman, who provided computer assistance above and beyond the call of duty. Other people who offered friendship and support are Carol Matt, Sue D'Aoust, Jefferson Saunders, and Glen Amerine.

Thanks to my aunts Esther Brown O'Shea and Merlyn Albert, who not only continue to set a splendid example for me of long-term vitality, but also generously gave me the use of the Discovery Bay duplex during the time I needed a private retreat to complete the first draft of this book.

I'm particularly delighted to be back with my New World Library family. Special thanks to my editor, Carol LaRusso; to publisher Marc Allen; and to Marjorie Conte, Sandra LaRusso, and all the other wonderful people at New World who make such beautiful books.

About the Author

ROBERTA JEAN BRYANT, the author of *Anybody Can Write —
A Playful Approach*, was educated in the libraries of the West.
She has raised four children and has written many published
articles and stories. As owner of her own business, Bryant
Ideas, she serves as a midwife for many published writers. Jean
is an idea person—a powerful and lively communicator whose
down-to-earth honesty and warm sense of humor have inspired and encouraged creative people for nearly twenty-five
years. She has been called "a powerhouse of joyful inspiration
in the dance of life."

Jean welcomes your comments and questions. For information about Jean's workshops, classes, or lectures, contact
her at:

P. O. Box 31282, Seattle, WA 98103
(206) 328-2670